--------21 WAYS TO

Divorce Proof

YOUR MARRIAGE

21 WAYS TO

Divorce Proof

YOUR MARRIAGE

Your Personal Guide to Creating a Strong and
Happy Marriage That Will Stand the Test of Time

DARREN & DONNA MCNEES

Blue Sail Publishing, Inc.

ISBN-13: 978-0-9721903-6-7
ISBN-10: 0-9721903-6-8

Printed in the United States of America

Dedicated to building strong
and happy marriages that will
stand the test of time.

CONTENTS

INTRODUCTION

I t has been said that life is a long strand of opportunities. Each and every day we have the opportunity to make decisions, choices that will affect the course of the day and ultimately our lives. This is true because every decision we make and every action we take has consequences either good or bad. Even the decision to do nothing has its consequences. While it may seem obvious that good decisions lead to positive results whereas bad decisions lead to negative results, it isn't always obvious in the moment to know which choice is the right choice.

That's what *21 Ways to Divorce Proof Your Marriage* is all about—helping you to make the right decisions and take the appropriate actions regarding your marital relationship. By doing so you will be amazed by the positive results you'll experience. Often the smallest adjustment to how you interact with your spouse can lead to dramatic results, improving your marriage in ways that you may have never even imagined.

Think of *21 Ways to Divorce Proof Your Marriage* as more than just a way to keep you out of divorce court. Think of it as a tool that you can use to literally transform your marriage and quite possibly change your life forever.

> "The greatest discovery of my generation
> is that man can alter his life simply
> by altering his attitude of mind."
> — William James

As you begin to read through this book, do so with an open mind and a receptive attitude. Avoid the temptation to think, "I already know that." Instead, reflect on each point and really let it sink in. Ask yourself how you can better apply this information to your marriage and your life.

By doing so, you'll set the stage for great things to happen!

So let's begin…

CHAPTER 1

KNOW
THE
TRUTH

"There are two ways to be fooled:
One is to believe what isn't so; the
other is to refuse to believe what is so."
— Soren Kierkegaard

The shocking truth about marriage is that if you are not actively working on improving your relationship, it will deteriorate over time. At any given moment, your marriage is either getting better or it's getting worse; there is no in-between.

A lot of married people don't realize or understand this simple truth. They go from day to day doing what they've always done and assume that everything will be fine. Sure, many of them know that they have problems in their marriage (who doesn't?) and that they and/or their spouse aren't as happy as they would like to be, but they aren't too worried because they figure things will eventually work out.

Then all of a sudden they wake up one day to discover that things are much worse than they had thought. A young man is crushed after he finds out that his wife of seven years is having an affair. A middle-aged woman is devastated after her husband tells her that he wants a divorce.

Men and women by the thousands are heart-broken when they hear their spouse say, "I don't love you anymore." And the statement that we hear the most from these people is, "I never thought it would happen to me."

How can this happen? How can so many people let their marriages fall apart? Well, it's not that they just "let" their marriage fall apart, it's that they don't "realize" that their marriage is falling apart.

If you were to gain six pounds per year, you may not even notice it at first. Since you look at yourself in the mirror every day, you can't see the daily changes (0.02 pounds per day).

After a while you can't help but notice that you're putting on a few extra pounds. Every year or two you buy clothes that are a little bigger, but the change seems harmless enough. Then, ten years down the road, you come across a picture of yourself ten years earlier. You're shocked! You take out a recent photo, compare the two and say, "Man—I've gotten fat!"

You didn't gain sixty pounds the day you looked at the earlier photo. Likewise, people don't "all of a sudden" have an affair, fall out of love or want a divorce.

> "To keep a lamp burning,
> we have to keep putting oil in it."
> — Mother Teresa

For dinner one evening you decide to have a delicious hot pizza. When it's done baking you pull it out of the oven and start to cut it when the phone rings.

You take the call in the other room and before you know it, twenty minutes have passed. By the time you get back to your pizza, it's stone cold. The only way to keep a pizza hot is to keep applying heat to it. Turn off the heat and the pizza gets cold.

Your marriage works the same way. The only way to keep it strong is to continually learn and do what it takes to make it so.

You Don't Have to Be a Statistic!

The other day I (Darren) was talking to a manager of a health club who told me that he was waiting to get called back to his "real job" in the telecommunications industry. He was studying heating and air-conditioning and told me that with this new knowledge added to what he already knew, he would always be employed.

On my way out, I mentioned that one way to increase his chances of not being laid off again was to start his own business. He very quickly said, "That's too risky—ninety-five percent of all businesses fail within the first five years."

While that statistic may be true, his logic was flawed.

Here he was waiting for a call-back from a company that let him go a year and a half ago. He felt that it was less risky to put his financial future in the hands of a company that had already demonstrated that they could let him go at any time without as much as a warning.

> Maybe it's just me, but if he started a business and it later failed, couldn't he still get a job as a manager of a health club?

Ninety-five percent of new businesses may indeed fail. So what! Who said he had to be one of the ninety-five percent? Why not learn how to be among the five percent that succeed? Why not study and apply the successful habits of the five percent instead of unknowingly following the unsuccessful habits of the ninety-five percent?

Thank goodness for the many men and women throughout history who didn't pay attention to statistics, but rather followed their hearts and pursued their dreams. Look around you right now and you'll notice that virtually everything you see was manufactured by a company started by someone who ignored the statistics or at the very least decided to be part of the five percent.

So what does this business story have to do with your marriage? Well, there's another statistic floating around that can be potentially harmful to your marriage if you're not careful. It's the overused and unsubstantiated divorce statistic that has been talked about for years. You know the one, "Fifty percent of marriages end in divorce."

Don't you find it odd that the number never changes? Wouldn't you think that over time the percentage would change to perhaps fifty-five percent or forty-five percent? No, the number almost everyone has used for a long time now is fifty percent—a magical number that is somehow fixed for all of time.

According to pollster Louis Harris, *"The idea that half of American marriages are doomed is one of the most specious pieces of statistical nonsense ever perpetuated in modern times. It all began when the Census Bureau noted that during one year, there were*

2.4 million marriages and 1.2 million divorces. Someone did the math without calculating the 54 million marriages already in existence, and presto, a ridiculous but quotable statistic was born. Only one out of eight marriages will end in divorce. In any given year, only two percent of existing marriages will break up."

As a matter of fact, the rate of divorce per year per 1,000 people in the U.S. has been declining since 1981 and is now at its lowest level since 1970. The future for marriage in America is looking very bright for those who decide to make it so. And thanks to marriage retreats, marriage experts, relationship books, tapes and videos and the Internet, people who want to improve their marriages can find excellent advice from any number of sources.

But unfortunately the misleading fifty percent statistic is still causing a lot of harm. This is true because of the psychological influence factor known as *social proof*. Social proof is basically a means by which we determine what is correct by finding out what others think is correct. One example of social proof is the best seller list. If a book hits the best seller list, more people will buy it, assuming that it must be good because a lot of other people bought it.

Social proof also works in the reverse direction. If we aren't careful, the bombardment of negative bad news from the media outlets can have a profoundly negative impact on our lives.

A person struggling in his or her marriage can become very vulnerable to this kind of negative input. He or she hears of several celebrities who are splitting up, then sees similar reports on the cover of the grocery store tabloids and then remembers hearing that fifty percent of marriages end in divorce. Under these circumstances it's easy for this person to lose hope and think, "If so many people are doing it, then it must be okay for me to do it as well."

If this same person thought that only two percent of existing marriages were ending in divorce, they would be a lot less likely to throw in the towel and more apt to do what it took to make things better.

With all that said, let's pretend for a moment that fifty percent of marriages end in divorce. So what! How does that affect *your* marriage? Who said you had to be in the failing half? You don't have to be a statistic!

The next time you read or hear someone say that fifty percent of marriages end in divorce, just smile and say to yourself, "I know the truth, and I *choose* to make my marriage great!"

CHAPTER 2

DON'T
BE
NAÏVE

"Almost no one is foolish enough to
imagine that he automatically deserves
great success in any field of activity;
yet almost everyone believes that he
automatically deserves success in marriage."
— Sydney J. Harris

L et's face it. No one enters into marriage thinking
that it will end in divorce or that they or their spouse
will have an affair. Most people truly believe that their
marriage will last forever. "It will never happen to me," is a
common statement made by many married couples today.
And that's a very healthy attitude to have as long as you're
taking the steps necessary to insure that it doesn't happen
to you.

The key thing to remember is that no one on this planet
is immune to divorce and/or an affair—no one. That doesn't
mean that you have to live in fear or become jealous or
paranoid. It just means that you have to be very aware of
your surroundings and the happiness level of both your and

your mate.

Don't assume that just because you think your marriage is good your spouse feels the same way. Just as a chain is only as strong as its weakest link, a marriage is only as strong as the lesser of the two opinions.

Here's a common scenario played out in the lives of couples all over the world. One of the partners thinks the marriage is fine. For the most part their needs are being met and they are relatively content with the way things are.

Meanwhile their mate is living in quiet desperation, completely unhappy with the state of the marriage. They may complain or voice their opinion now and then, but their petition isn't taken seriously. They are hurt or lonely and their partner doesn't even know it. They aren't getting what they want, need and deserve from their partner.

Then one day the wounded party innocently grabs a bite to eat with an acquaintance of the opposite sex from work, church or the health club. They have a great time, laughing and making small talk, so they decide to meet for coffee the next morning. They almost immediately become good friends and even start sharing things about their personal lives, including their marriage.

Through this new friendship, the wounded person starts to receive what they so desperately need but aren't getting from their spouse. They receive undivided attention, compliments, praise, acceptance and encouragement. They are treated kindly and with respect. The more time they spend together, the closer they become. One thing leads to another and a full-blown affair begins.

What many people don't realize is that an affair isn't always about sex—at least, it doesn't start out that way.

An affair starts like many marriages do, as a friendship. Also know that an affair doesn't just hurt the one who has been betrayed. It isn't uncommon for us to hear from the person who has been in an affair explaining how they can't seem to pick up the pieces of a broken life. They are in so much pain and wish that they could start all over again.

Make sure that you don't fall prey to this tragic event. This can be accomplished by avoiding being alone with someone of the opposite sex. That means no late night work projects, no on-going lunch meetings, no coffee dates, etc.

The best way to keep from falling into a hole is to stay as far away from the hole as possible. That may seem like "old-fashioned" or impractical advice, but only you can determine how important your marriage is and what you will be willing to do to keep it strong and healthy.

As soon as you are done reading this paragraph, take out a piece of paper and rate your marriage on a scale from one to ten, with one being that you are ready to file for divorce and ten being that you couldn't imagine a better marriage.

Then go to your partner when the timing is right and you have their full attention. Tell them that you love them and that you have a very important question to ask them and that you want them to be completely open and honest. Let them know that you will in no way get mad at their answer, and that you just want to know the truth. Then ask them how they would rate the marriage.

The lower of the two scores is the correct score. Now you have a better idea of where you stand. Any score less than eight should be taken seriously and even that score can be improved upon with a little extra effort on your part.

We would also highly recommend that you and your spouse take the short quiz at UltimateRelationshipQuiz.com.

CHAPTER 3

HAVE THE COURAGE TO BUILD A GREAT MARRIAGE

"Courage is the most important of all
virtues, because without it we can't
practice any other virtue with consistency."
— Maya Angelou

C ourage is an attribute that is difficult to find today. Too many people are afraid to rock the boat, go against the flow, stand up for what they believe in, follow their dreams and press on when things get tough. They have no fight, no driving passion to do what they know deep down is right. And in the end, that kind of existence leaves them feeling less than fulfilled.

"Life shrinks or expands
in proportion to one's courage."
— Anaïs Nin

Without courage, life is only half lived. It is courage, not just desire, that will enable you to live the life that you want to live. It takes courage to achieve success in any area of your life. It takes courage to pursue your dreams and reach your goals. It takes courage to be happy. And yes, it takes courage to have an awesome marriage.

> "I believe half the unhappiness in life
> comes from people being afraid
> to go straight at things."
> — William J. Lock

It's only natural to want to avoid conflict, take the easy way out or the path of least resistance. It is courage that causes us to see things the way that they are and to do what is necessary to improve the situation. William J.H. Boetcher noted that *"No man will succeed unless he is ready to face and overcome difficulties, and is prepared to assume responsibilities."*

Denial will not improve the quality of your life. Ignoring or running away from your problems will not make them disappear. Blaming other people, your circumstances or your past will not bring you freedom.

So what does courage have to do with having and maintaining a great marriage?

A marriage, like any relationship, isn't always a bed of roses. Challenges and difficulties come up and need to be addressed and resolved. Not realizing that things aren't the way they should be is ignorance. Knowing that things aren't right and failing to address and resolve the issue is cowardice. Confucius once said, *"To know what is right and not do it is the worst cowardice."*

"There is a time when to avoid trouble
is to store up trouble, and when to
seek for a lazy and a cowardly peace
is to court a still greater danger."
— William Barclay

Are there things about your relationship that you would like to discuss with your partner, but you're too afraid to bring them up? Do you go out of your way to avoid conflict or confrontation in an attempt to "keep the peace?" Do you openly share your goals, dreams and desires with your spouse? Do you regularly discuss your finances, including spending habits, investment strategies and savings plans? Do you talk about the emotional and physical aspects of your relationship, including affection, respect, sex, playfulness and encouragement?

"Because a fellow has failed once or twice
or a dozen times, you don't want to set him
down as a failure till he's dead or loses his
courage—and that's the same thing."
— George Horace Lorimer

The bottom line is this—sometimes you have to fight for what you want. Too many people just lay down and die when things seem hopeless. They mentally and emotionally prepare themselves for the worst and in doing so they receive the worst. It is at times like this that you need to gather your strength and stand up for what you believe in.

"Happy the man who ventures boldly
to defend what he holds dear."
— Ovid

If your relationship is in serious trouble, don't shut down emotionally, crawl into a corner and just wait for the divorce papers to arrive—**stand up and fight for your marriage**. Continue to consistently meet your spouse's specific love needs (as will be discussed later) even if your needs aren't being met. Be the spouse that you know you should be even if you don't think that it will make one bit of difference. As George Eliot noted, *"Any coward can fight a battle when he's sure of winning."* The true test of courage is to do what's right regardless of the perceived outcome.

> "Whatever course you decide upon,
> there is always someone to tell you that you
> are wrong. There are always difficulties arising which
> tempt you to believe that your critics are
> right. To map out a course of action and
> follow it to an end requires...courage."
> — Ralph Waldo Emerson

It takes courage to follow your dreams when those around you think you're crazy or tell you that you can't do it. It takes courage to call on a customer for the seventh time when all previous attempts have failed. It takes courage to turn a strained relationship into an awesome one. And perhaps most of all, it takes courage to take an honest look at your life and accept the things you can't change and change the things you can.

Courage isn't something that you were either born with or without. It isn't just found in heroes, nor is it the absence of fear. Courage is a choice. It's the decision to venture, persevere and withstand difficulty and fear.

*"The greatest test of courage on earth
is to bear defeat without losing heart."*
— Robert G. Ingersoll

It's impossible to be an active participant in life without experiencing challenges and difficulties. When times are tough and hope seems to fade, the boldest plans render the best results. Be bold; be strong, for without courage life is only half lived.

Last, but not least—have the courage to believe in yourself. You have what it takes to do more than you could have ever imagined. There is a German proverb that states, *"Great things are done more through courage than through wisdom."* Don't let your potential lay dormant—believe in yourself, be bold and take action!

CHAPTER 4

ACT
AS
THOUGH

"Everything in life that we really
accept undergoes a change."
— Katherine Mansfield

T he topic that we're about to discuss was most likely
not taught to you by your parents or grandparents.
It isn't something that you learned in school and you
may not have read about it in personal-growth materials.
It's a concept that when understood and applied has the
potential to transform many areas of your life, especially your
marriage. Like many of life's lessons, it's simple yet
challenging to apply, requiring a conscious and deliberate
effort.

If you've been married for any length of time you realize
that you can't change your spouse. If you've tried, you've
most likely ended up frustrated, angry or disappointed.

There are, however, numerous ways that you can change the dynamics of your relationship—to greatly improve your marriage without "directly" changing your spouse. By first changing yourself (your outlook, attitude, thoughts and behavior), you set the stage for positive change to take place. This change can even include an "indirect" change in your spouse.

When we talk about direct change we're referring to any and all things that you may do to try and change your spouse—things like whining, pouting, threatening, demanding, nagging, manipulative or passive aggressive behavior, pulling back or withholding certain things like love, affection, physical intimacy, etc. Some of these methods may render small or temporary results, but more times than not, they just lead to a lot of frustration for you and your partner and may even lead to arguing or fighting.

Direct change is something that takes place, if at all, in an attempt to appease the person making the request.

Indirect change happens as an automatic response (consciously or subconsciously, voluntarily or involuntarily) to outside stimuli. This kind of change is something that the other person wants to do or feels compelled to do.

It's kind of like the difference between demanding change and inspiring change.

Sending the Right Signals

Have you ever said or thought a statement like this, "She's saying all the right things, but I can see right through her"? What did you mean by that? What was it that you "saw"? Or have you ever felt really uncomfortable around someone even though you didn't have a reason for feeling that way?

What was it that made you feel uncomfortable? Deep down you sensed something, didn't you? It may not have been something visible or something you could put your finger on, but for some reason you knew something wasn't quite right.

We all give off vibrations or signals to those around us. These signals tell people what we think about a situation, what we think about ourselves and what we think of them. None of us are as good an actor as we may think we are. We may fool some of the people some of the time, but more times than not, people see right through us. Some of us are so transparent and/or open that the phrase, "He wears his feelings on his shirt sleeve" fits us to a tee.

These vibrations or signals can attract things into our lives or repel things away from us. Donna is a great example of this. When she used to work in downtown Chicago, she would take the train into work. On several occasions she would have complete strangers tell her their whole life story or some of the major events that were going on in their lives. Some of these people would even be amazed themselves and say things like, "I haven't told anyone that before, not even my husband."

What would cause a complete stranger to open up to her like that? Somehow these people could sense that Donna was an accepting, non-judgmental and caring person. They felt safe and at ease around her.

When you hold a less than positive image of your partner in your mind, you unknowingly and automatically send those negative signals to him or her. They pick up those signals through their sixth sense, store them in their subconscious mind and act or react toward you in a way that is congruent with those signals. If the "vibes" that you're sending out are ones of judgment, rejection or disapproval, then your partner will be less willing to try and please you.

Since an environment filled with judgment, rejection or disapproval is extremely uncomfortable and undesirable; your spouse may even try to avoid you all together. They may spend extra time at work, more time with their friends, more time playing sports or working on a hobby or any other activity that gets them away from this uncomfortable environment. Or maybe they don't leave physically, but retreat or shut down emotionally. Whatever the method of avoidance, one thing's for sure; this is not the way to foster a close, healthy relationship.

When you think positive thoughts about your partner, you unknowingly and automatically send those positive signals to him or her. They pick up those signals and act or react toward you in a way that is congruent with those signals. If the "vibes" that you're sending out are ones of love, acceptance and approval, then your partner will be much more willing to try and please you. And by doing this you will have created an environment for positive change to take place. As Carl Jung observed, *"We cannot change anything unless we accept it. Condemnation does not liberate, it oppresses."*

Now for the main point of this chapter:

To increase the chances of getting what you want, act as though what you want has already happened.

In the context of your marriage that means that you should treat your spouse as though they were already the kind of person that you want them to be. If you are willing to do this, you'll be very impressed with the results.

When you think and act toward your spouse in this way, there is no room for judgment, rejection or disapproval. In time, your partner will become more like the positive image that you hold in your mind. This happens in part because of two reasons:

1. You have created a loving, accepting and safe environment for positive change to take place. It's kind of like planting seed in rich fertile soil versus throwing seed on a hard dirt path.

2. People tend to live up to our expectations of them.

This is what we mean by indirectly changing your spouse.

Acting as though what you want has already happened isn't a condition that will happen automatically—you have to work at it. You have to decide that this is what you want to do and continually keep your thoughts in check because if you don't your thought patterns will drift right back to your old way of thinking.

When you hold a picture in your mind of what you want, believing that you have already received it, you begin to attract that very thing into your life.

As an example, you probably know someone who has a low self-image and feels like they're undeserving of the best that life has to offer. What kind of people do they attract into their life? People who take advantage of them and treat them poorly. They send out signals that it's okay for people to treat them that way. What we are suggesting is that you do the very opposite—only send out what you want more of in your life.

*   To receive more love, you have to love yourself and become more loving.

- Become more accepting of others, overlooking their faults and you'll attract more acceptance into your life.

- The less you judge, the less you'll be judged.

- Think positive, uplifting and empowering thoughts and you'll attract good into your life.

- Think and act as though what you want has already happened and you'll greatly increase the odds that you'll receive it.

Be Patient

Some positive results may happen quickly, others will take time, consistency and patience. One thing's for sure, when you start to think and act more positively toward others and your circumstances; your whole outlook on the world will change for the better. And if that's all that happens, your new mental practice will have been well worth the effort.

CHAPTER 5

IDENTIFY AND MEET YOUR SPOUSE'S SPECIFIC "LOVE NEEDS"

"Happy marriages begin when we marry
the ones we love, and they blossom
when we love the ones we marry."
— Tom Mullen

W hen you got married you weren't given a marriage manual that explained in great detail how to build an awesome relationship with your spouse. You probably weren't told that you and your partner each had different and unique "love needs" that needed to be identified and met in order to experience a mutually fulfilling relationship. You weren't taught how to effectively handle conflict or how to best make your concerns known.

You may not have learned that men and women listen with different sides of their brain, interpret conversations differently and speak a different "love language." You may not have discovered how the differences in your personalities and upbringing factor into your relationship. You probably weren't told that holding unforgiveness toward someone else could actually harm the relationship that you have with your spouse.

And the list goes on and on.

Not knowing these things can lead to a lot of frustration, loneliness and pain. It can make you feel like your situation is hopeless, that your partner will never change and/or that marriage doesn't work.

A marriage or committed relationship is very complex, yet the answer to improving it is relatively simple. How do we know that it's simple? Because when couples finally discover the answers and apply them to their marriage, their relationship starts to improve almost immediately. It's almost like removing a thorn so that your finger can heal.

Unfortunately, a lot of people just assume that their partner's wants and needs are the same as their own. Even couples who actively search for ways to improve their relationship can be lead astray by well meaning friends and family, even professionals who may or may not understand this critically important topic. The following are just a couple examples:

1. Giving your spouse what "you" need. "I give and give to my wife, but she doesn't give me anything in return," says a frustrated man who is ready to divorce his wife. He invites his wife to come golfing with him, watch the game, etc., but she isn't interested. He is encouraging and supportive, yet his wife's reactions are neutral at best. He wants to show her his love and affection through physical intimacy, but she rejects him time and again. He suggests that they go to counseling; she makes it clear that he can go if he wants, but she won't because he is the one with the problem, not her.

"I shower my husband with affection and write him love notes, but he doesn't respond in kind," says a lonely woman who feels like she is living in an empty relationship. She tells her husband how much she appreciates him and always wants to know what he is thinking.

These all sound like good things, and they are, but they may not be the things that their spouses need from them. They are practicing the common mistake of giving their respective partners what "they" need instead of giving their partners what it is that "their partners" need. And they have no idea that this is what they are doing.

When a woman doesn't receive the kind of affection that she needs from her husband (which could include kisses, hugs, tender words like, "I love you," compliments, flowers, cards, love notes, touches, gifts, quality time, flirting, etc.) she is less likely to want to be physically intimate with him.

If a woman is constantly nagging her husband, telling him how to do things and complaining when he does something wrong, he is less likely to honor, appreciate and respect her. When she plays with him and takes an interest in his interests, he is more open to talking with her and listening to her concerns.

In short, if you aren't meeting your spouse's specific "love needs," then the likelihood of you getting *your* love needs met will be greatly reduced. They are intertwined—it's a matter of cause and effect.

Love Needs are simply the conditions that must be met in your relationship in order for you and your partner to feel loved and accepted by each other and for both of you to feel good about the relationship. So, unless and until you learn exactly what it is that your partner wants and needs from you, your relationship will never be as good as it can be.

2. Taking the wrong approach or listening to the wrong advice. A lady came up to us after one of our marriage improvement seminars to ask for advice regarding her marriage. She had been married for over thirty years and was experiencing problems in her marriage. She and her husband had gone to counseling and she wanted to know what we thought of the advice she was given.

Their counselor suggested that they each make a list of all of the things that bothered them about each other. When the list was complete, they were to meet to discuss the items on the list in an effort to resolve their problems. That kind of logic may make sense on the surface, but telling your spouse what you don't like about him or her is not a great way to start building a healthy marriage.

We suggested the exact opposite. We told her that she and her husband should make a list of all of the things that they liked about each other and that each of them should read from their respective lists when they were alone. (Your assignment for the week is to do the same.)

We asked how she thought it would make her feel if they spent the better part of an hour telling each other what they liked and appreciated about each other. She smiled and said that it would feel wonderful!

The advice she was given was common, and it's the kind of thing that we naturally gravitate toward when things aren't the way we would like them to be. How often do we tell our partner how they should do things differently, what we disapprove of and how they should change? On the surface this may seem like a good way to get what we want, but little do we know that the exact opposite is true.

One of our strongest basic human needs is to be accepted and one of our biggest fears is rejection. If the lady mentioned above had taken the advice of her counselor, do you think that she and her husband would have felt accepted or rejected by each other?

You become healthy by focusing on health, not by focusing on disease. The same thing is true with your marriage. Your marriage becomes healthier by focusing on what you can do to improve it, not by focusing on all of the things that are wrong with it. And a good place to start is to focus on all of the things that you like and appreciate about your spouse.

Acceptance will set the stage for positive change and improve the quality of your relationship, whereas rejection will push you further apart.

Therefore, it's very important that you discover exactly what has to happen in order for your partner to "feel" accepted and loved by you. It's a little different for everyone and not getting it right can cause a lot of problems in a marriage.

To help point you in the right direction, we've divided love into the following four categories:

1. **Seeing love**

2. **Feeling love**

3. **Hearing love**

4. **Experiencing love**

Seeing Love

Some people need to see love in order to know that you love them. To them, love is more about what you do than what you say. They know that you love them when you do things for them. They feel loved when you do acts of service like taking out the trash, washing the dishes and the clothes, working to bring home money to support the family, cooking dinner, mowing the lawn, cleaning the house, making them a cup of tea, etc. Others feel loved by your acts of affection like giving them flowers, gifts, cards and love notes, etc.

If they don't "see" love, they may not feel that you love them or they may not be fulfilled and happy with your relationship. This may not be true, but it's their perception and perception is all that matters.

Feeling Love

These people sense love through touch. They feel loved when you hold their hand, put your arm around them, give them a hug or a kiss, touch their shoulder, stroke their hair, give them a back or foot rub, etc. The more you touch them the more love they feel from you. Sex can also fall into this category, but it doesn't have to. We will talk more about that a little later.

Hearing Love

These people need to hear that you love them. They know that you love them by your praise, encouragement, compliments, admiration, respect, appreciation and acceptance. Nothing makes them feel better than hearing things like, "You look great," "You're so talented," "I'm very proud of how you handled that," "I truly appreciate all that you do for me and the family," "You're such a good dad/mom," "Hang in there, you'll figure it out, you're awesome," and of course, "I love you."

Experiencing Love

These people feel loved by what you do together as a couple. They feel loved when you go for walks together, go out to eat, go to a play or a movie, play with each other, go camping, watch the sun set, ride bikes, have date nights, go for weekend get-a-ways, go on a vacation, etc. And let's not forget three of the most important relationship building experiences, talking, listening and investing a lot of time with each other. Nothing can replace time. Your time is one of the most valuable gifts that you could ever give another person.

What About Sex?

Sex probably deserves its own category. It's not just something that you do for your mate or a tactile experience or something that you experience together. For those whose primary love need is sex, not fulfilling this need can be just as dangerous to a marriage as not talking to each other, not spending any alone time with each other or never telling your spouse that you love him or her.

To this person, rejecting sex is like rejecting him or her— he or she may take that as a sign that you don't find him or her desirable, that you don't love him or her or that you would rather be with someone else. We realize that that may sound extreme, but that's how serious love needs are. If you don't meet your spouse's specific love needs, it leaves them with an empty feeling regarding your relationship.

And if you're not careful, someone else may fill that empty feeling. That's how many affairs happen. Someone else enters the picture and fills the love need that's been missing in the relationship. As we mentioned earlier, many if not most affairs start off as friendships and grow into much more as both parties begin to meet each other's need for affection, meaningful communication, trust, acceptance, admiration, respect, appreciation, focused time with each other, etc.

How Do You Know That You Are Demonstrating True Love?

Mature love isn't just a feeling. Feelings come and go and change all the time. If your love is dependent upon how you feel or what someone does or doesn't do, then that isn't true love.

Love is derived from the Latin word *libere*, which means "to please." Not knowing that simple truth can cause one to feel frustration, loneliness and emotional coldness, and it can even lead one to believe that he or she has "fallen out of love."

Notice that the definition says "to please" and not "to receive pleasure." That is a very important distinction. In our marital relationships we often put the cart in front of the horse and then wonder why we aren't going anywhere. If you demonstrate the *actions* of love toward your mate, the *feelings* of love will follow. That strategy worked for you before and it will work for you again. It's a simple case of cause and effect.

True love isn't selfish or conditional, yet that is often how we act in our relationship. We will give to our spouse, but when we don't receive what we want in return, we pull back and give less. Our attitude toward them changes and consequently the way we act toward them changes as well. This is a big mistake. Discontinuing the acts of love will only make things worse and may ultimately cause you and/or your spouse to want out of the marriage.

Four Steps to Get More Love (What You Want and Need) from Your Partner

Step 1: Find out how your spouse needs to receive love. If your spouse is open to the idea, have them read the four categories of love listed above and ask them which one(s) they relate with. Keep in mind that no one fits into just one category. Have your spouse list the things that are important to them and write them down. If your partner isn't willing to participate, you can sometimes tell what their primary love needs are by paying attention to what they complain about the most.

If your mate complains that you spend too much time at work or too much time with your friends, watching TV, playing golf, fishing or working on a hobby, then time is one of their primary love needs. What they are really saying is, "I wish that you would spend more time with me." If your spouse says that you never listen to them, that you don't understand them or that you don't care about what they are thinking or about their opinions, then communication is the missing ingredient. Listen very carefully to your spouse's complaints as well as their requests, and before long you'll get a pretty good idea of what they need from you.

While it is true that identifying and meeting your spouse's specific "love needs" is absolutely essential to achieving a mutually fulfilling marriage, we still cannot forget the ancient words of wisdom, "Ask and you will receive."

So much frustration could be avoided in a marriage if we would just tell our partner what it is that we want and need from him or her instead of expecting our partner to be able to figure it out on their own or read our mind. Instead we set ourselves up for disappointment time and time again.

Let's say that you want your spouse to take you someplace special for your upcoming anniversary. The day comes and you receive a nice card and a heartfelt "I love you," but nothing more. Whose fault is it that you didn't go somewhere special? Or you're walking with your partner and you would like to hold hands. Do you wait for him or her to take your hand, or do you initiate the action? When you need a hug from your mate, do you ask for one?

Some people think that if they have to tell their spouse what to do, then the act isn't sincere or romantic. They want the other person to figure it out on their own or to be spontaneous.

Write this next sentence down because it's very important.

If you want to have a mutually fulfilling relationship with your mate, then you need to stop expecting him or her to be able to read your mind, because he or she can't!

That's right, your spouse can't read your mind, so stop thinking that they should know what to do, what to say, what they did to offend you, etc.

Don't drop hints or beat around the bush, either. That doesn't work. We know that this may sound a little harsh or rub you the wrong way, but we're trying to help you to have the best marriage possible. To do so, you may need to think differently than you have in the past.

If your shoulder muscles were really tense and you needed a back rub, would you wait for your partner to come over to you and start rubbing your shoulders (and then get upset if they don't), or would you ask him or her to give you a back rub? Why is it then that we have different expectations and take on a different attitude when it comes to some of our other wants and needs?

Some of our marital arguments are a direct result of us assuming that our spouse should know what to do, and then getting upset with them when they don't do it.

Avoid this unnecessary drama by simply telling your spouse exactly what you want, how often you want it, and if possible, tell them what it will mean to you and how it will make you feel. Give your mate as much detail as possible. That will help them to remember to repeat the things you appreciate in the future.

It is especially important for men to know "why" these things are so important, because to him, they are just things. He needs to know what they represent and to be told the meaning and feelings behind them. Be patient, you may have to tell your spouse several times before it becomes something that your spouse does on his or her own.

Now, we're not trying to let anyone off the hook. It's still "your" responsibility to find out what your spouse needs and then give it to him or her and vice versa, but often you have to be the one to tell your mate what it is that you want and need. "You have not because you ask not" is not just a catchy phrase, but rather a principle to be applied to every aspect of our lives.

Step 2: Close your eyes and envision your spouse meeting your love needs and treating you the way you want to be treated. This is very powerful because thoughts are things. You can manifest things into your life just by thinking about them. Successful people in all walks of life practice this technique.

Athletes close their eyes and envision themselves running the perfect race. Business people envision the success and growth of their company from the very beginning. Peak performers hold a picture in their mind of exactly what their life will be like in the future right down to the smallest detail.

> "Change your thoughts
> and you change your world."
> — Norman Vincent Peale

What you think about the most grows; it expands to become a bigger part of your life. Whatever you think about attracts more of the same into your life.

If you think thoughts of anger, you attract anger. If you think peaceful loving thoughts, peace and love show up in your life. Think scarcity and you experience scarcity. Think abundance and abundance finds you, opportunities are attracted to you. That's how the universe operates.

> "The life each of us lives is the life
> within the limits of our own thinking.
> To have life more abundant, we must
> think in limitless terms of abundance."
> — Thomas Dreier

So when you think about your spouse, think only about the things that you want to experience in your life. When a negative thought enters your mind, immediately get rid of it and replace it with a positive one, because *"He who cannot change the very fabric of his thoughts will never be able to change reality."* — Anwar Sadat

Step 3: Speak only good things about your partner. Too many people run around to all of their friends and tell them how unfairly they're being treated or what terrible thing their spouse did this time. This is poison to your relationship and it has to stop immediately.

Thoughts are very powerful, but when those thoughts become words, they carry even more power. When you speak, you hear your own words and those words strengthen your belief in what you're saying. And what you believe about your spouse affects how you act toward them, which in turn affects how they act toward you.

There's no doubt that you'll find plenty of friends, family members, therapists and counselors that will agree with you and encourage you to quit, to give up.

It's a very rare gift indeed to have someone in your life who will encourage you to succeed, to press through the difficult times and come out the winner, and who isn't afraid to tell you the truth, even if it isn't what you want to hear. So be very careful who you talk to and even more careful who you listen to.

Step 4: Treat your mate as though he or she is the person you envisioned in step two. This is literally a relationship transforming experience. As discussed in Chapter 4, you can't directly change your spouse. If you've tried you know how frustrating and useless that exercise is. But you can indirectly change your spouse through your thoughts, attitude and actions toward him or her.

Over time, people have the tendency to live up to your expectations of them. If you expect the worst you often get it, but when you expect great things to happen it's as though you're sending them an invisible challenge to live up to your expectations. And often they rise to the occasion.

> "It is the nature of man to rise to greatness
> if greatness is expected of him."
> — John Steinbeck

The principles discussed in this chapter aren't just wishful thinking or things that we made up one day as we were gazing at the stars. These principles have been taught for thousands of years and proven through modern day studies.

One such study was conducted at a grade school where the teacher was informed that certain students were exceptionally brilliant, but that they needed to be challenged or they would get bored and lose interest. What the teacher didn't know was that these kids were only average students and that she was part of an experiment studying how well students perform when they are expected to do well.

At the end of the semester these so-called "brilliant" kids did indeed perform brilliantly. They actually became the kind of students that the teacher thought they were all along.

Follow these six steps and your relationship has no choice but to improve:

1. Make sure that you're giving your partner love in the way that he or she needs to receive love.

2. Give love unconditionally with no strings attached because that's what true love is.

3. When you think about your spouse, think only about what you like about him or her and picture your partner giving you love in the way that you need to be loved.

4. When talking about your mate, say only good things.

5. Treat you spouse as though they are already the person in Step 3.

6. Avoid people who speak poorly about their spouses. Spouse bashing is not an activity for you to take part in whether just listening or participating. You want the best out of life and to receive the best you have to surround yourself with the best. Spend time with people who you want to be more like, because that's exactly what will happen.

If you don't learn how to identify and meet your spouse's specific love needs, you can get re-married ten times and it won't make a bit a difference—no partner will be the right partner.

One of the Most Overlooked Needs

Marriage is much more than just a piece of paper or an elaborate ceremony or a joyous celebration. Marriage is a sacred pledge or commitment between two people to honor, respect, encourage and support one another. To be there for each other in good times and in bad, to lift each other up and to have each other's best interest in mind.

Even though through marriage the "two become one," that doesn't mean that you become the same person. You do share a very special spiritual, physical and emotional bond, but each of you still has your own set of unique skills, talents, abilities, goals, dreams and desires, which need to be met or expressed in order to experience fulfillment in life.

You may have an excellent relationship in every other area, but if you and/or your spouse has unfulfilled goals and dreams and/or unused skills and talents, then your marriage will never be as good or complete as it can be. In any close relationship, especially a marriage, it can be very easy to lose oneself in the relationship. This is especially true where one partner has a strong or dominate personality, is bossy or demanding, or is just plain selfish.

The most successful marriages are ones that run like a partnership not a dictatorship. With that in mind, it is extremely important that you and your partner meet on a regular basis to discuss not only "family" goals, but your individual goals, dreams and desires as well.

If for example your spouse expresses a desire to go to college, learn to play the piano, move to a different area or start a business, don't just dismiss the idea or rationalize it away by saying that you can't afford it, that it's not important or a priority, that it's too risky or that it will never work. Instead, put your heads together and figure out a way to make it work.

Never underestimate the importance of one's desires; they are there for a reason.

Make sure that you continually support and encourage your spouse to discover and pursue his or her dreams—to become the person they were meant to be. By doing so your spouse will become happier and more content, your relationship will improve and *your* life will become more joyous as well.

It is amazing how we can completely change the quality of our relationship simply by identifying and meeting our spouse's specific love needs.

CHAPTER 6

ELIMINATE YOUR MONEY PRESSURES

"I finally know what distinguishes man from other beasts: financial worries."
— Jules Renard

Most relationship books and many marriage counselors barely address the topic of money or even mention it at all. That's surprising given the fact that as many as ninety-five percent of arguments and fights in a marriage are over money issues.

As a matter of fact, many experts agree that the number one issue leading to divorce in America is money. According to a Lou Harris Poll, ninety-six percent of people lying awake at night are worrying about either finances or health.

There is no doubt that financial pressures can put a huge strain on your marriage. That's why the largest section in our 21-day marriage improvement program,

The 21 Day Marriage Makeover: How to transform your marriage into one filled with more love, affection, fun and happiness, is the money section. It's that important!

> "Money isn't the most important thing
> in life, but it's reasaonbly close to
> oxygen on the 'gotta have it' scale."
> -Zig Ziglar

And relieving your money pressures, paying off your debt, even creating financial abundance may be easier than you think. That is, as long as you know the key money principles and strategies that will take you from where you are to where you want to be.

In this chapter we'll first take a look at where it all begins—the thoughts and attitudes that you have toward money and those who have a lot of it. Then we'll give you some practical tips to help move you toward eliminating your money pressures.

If you're perfectly happy with your current financial situation or if having more money would just be a burden to you, then this chapter is not for you. You have our permission to jump to the next chapter.

If, however, you would like to rid yourself of money pressures, go on nicer vacations, be able to send your children to the university of your choice, or have more to give to your church or charity, then stay tuned for some insights that may include the missing ingredient that you've been looking for.

There is a reason why you aren't exactly where you want to be financially, and that reason may not be an obvious one. Some areas are relatively easy to identify, like poor spending habits, not paying yourself first (investing), lack of belief in yourself, pessimism or doubt, feelings of unworthiness, thinking that you aren't smart enough, talented enough, experienced enough or educated enough, etc. But often it's the areas of your life that you are unaware of, the thoughts and beliefs that operate on a subconscious level, that are the most harmful to your monetary success.

Think back to the first thoughts that you had about money when you were a child. What were your early experiences with money like? Were you taught lessons of abundance or scarcity? Did you learn that money will grow and be attracted to you if you treat it well, or did you learn that you better hold on tight to what you have if you don't want to lose it? Were you taught to look for sales or to look for opportunities?

What did your parents think and say about money and the people who had it? Were you taught that money was bad or that only greedy or mean people had a lot of it? Was money valued over people? Did you feel like your parent(s) cared more about making money than spending time with you? Was money a source of pain or pleasure in your home as a child?

These questions are very important because your early thoughts, beliefs and experiences about money can stay with you for the rest of your life, affecting every decision that you make regarding your finances. Added to that is the negative exposure we receive on an almost daily basis from movies, TV shows and the media portraying wealthy people as the bad guys.

Politicians promise that if you vote for them they will tax the undeserving rich and give that money to you. We look at Robin Hood as the hero and characterize the heads of business as tyrants running evil empires. We're at war, it's them against us—the rich against everyone else and the rich are winning.

It's no wonder so many people are struggling financially, can't seem to get ahead, or reach a certain level of success and then sabotage themselves. No one wants to be the bad guy.

As long as you have even the smallest negative associations about money, either consciously or unconsciously, you will never reach your full financial potential—regardless of how badly you want to. Your subconscious mind will not allow you to have what you view as bad or what you secretly despise.

- If you are in a financial hole and you can't see a way out...

- If you can't seem to get ahead no matter how hard you try...

- If every time you get ahead financially, something happens that puts you back at square one...

- If you don't have as much money invested as you had hoped you would at this stage in your life...

- If you keep getting passed over for promotions at work...

- If you can't seem to break bad spending habits...

...you may have linked money, attaining money or what it means to be a wealthy person with something negative or undesirable.

So how do you rewrite this negative mental programming? You do it by exchanging your negative associations for positive ones. And the way to start that process is to recognize money for what it really is. **Money is a tool.** That's all—nothing more and nothing less. It isn't good and it isn't bad. Sure, it can be used for good purposes or for bad ones, but it's your money and you can choose what you do with it.

How effective would an auto mechanic be without his tools? How about a plumber or an electrician? If money is a tool, how much more effective could you be if you had more of it? Would your child become a better athlete or musician if you hired a personal coach or instructor for him or her? If they were struggling in a certain subject at school, would a private tutor help? Will you send them to the best college or one that you can afford?

Would you like to help out your relatives who are struggling financially? Would your church or favorite charities be better off if you were better off? All of these things take money, a tool to be used to make life a little better.

Money in the hands of a good and generous person is a wonderful thing. The more they receive the more good they can do. It's okay to want more of a good thing!

A while back Darren taught a class on the psychological and spiritual aspects of money. After the class a young couple in their mid-thirties came up to him smiling from ear-to-ear, telling him that they finally got it.

They no longer felt like they had to make excuses or feel bad about their recent financial success. The wife had recently started her own business, which enabled them to build a new home and purchase a new truck. Her business was growing fast, but instead of being excited they started feeling a little guilty about their success (the beginning stages of self-sabotage).

They both grew up in poor families and had past negative money associations. When they heard the truth about money, they knew that it was okay to want and have it.

In essence, Darren gave them permission to make as much as they would like and know that it was a good thing to do. Today, they are pioneering churches out west.

Money—friend or foe, good or bad? What do you think? Because in the end, that's all that really matters.

As soon as you successfully identify and correct (if necessary) the thoughts, attitudes and beliefs that you have about money, you open yourself up to receive more of it. And that's a good thing. However, more money will not necessarily solve all your money problems. That's because money itself is rarely the root of the problem. Sure having a lot of money can make life easier, but only once you've solved the root money problem.

If you don't first address the "cause" of your money problems, more money can actually make things worse, a lot worse. Just ask the countless people who have filed for bankruptcy after winning the lottery. The more money you make, the more credit you'll be given, and the more credit you're given the deeper you can dig yourself in a hole.

The remainder of this chapter will focus on two practical steps that you can take to help eliminate your money pressures.

Step 1: Follow the rule of holes; when you find yourself in one, stop digging.

> *"Debt is a trap which man sets and baits himself, and then deliberately gets into."*
> — Josh Billings

If you're in debt—stop spending! Cut down your living expenses to "survival mode" and use the excess to pay down your debt as quickly as possible. That means buy only what you need.

Think of it this way—if you have $3,000 in credit card debt, every time that you pay your monthly cable/satellite TV bill, you're digging yourself further in debt. This is true because the payment you make for this unnecessary expense could have been used to pay down your credit card debt, and due to interest the payoff on the credit card increases with every passing day.

It's important that you're honest with yourself. Until your debt is paid off, everything that you spend money on is purchased with borrowed money—you don't really own it or at the very least you can't really afford it. The financially smart thing to do is to cancel your cable/satellite TV subscription, stop eating out, golfing, buying new clothes, etc. until your debt is paid in full. Then and only then is the money you spend 100 percent your own.

And by all means, DO NOT take out a "home equity" loan. Most people (typically banks) would have you believe that taking out a home equity loan is the smart thing to do. They encourage you to "pay off all of your high interest credit cards," "pay for your vacation," "add an addition to your home," "buy a new car" and " pay for your kid's college education" with their easy-to-get harmless little loan.

This may be stating the obvious, but a home equity loan is really a second mortgage. The reason banks are so willing to give you this money is because you're using your house as collateral. If for whatever reason you can't make your home equity loan payments for a couple months, they can foreclose on your home. That's right, they can take your house away all because you had to have or do whatever it was that you needed the money for. So instead of receiving late penalties (on credit cards for example) because you temporarily can't make the payments (unexpected job loss, medical expenses, etc.), they take away your home.

Pay off your debt with your income and by cutting back on unnecessary expenses, not by jeopardizing your house.

Step 2: Talk about your finances often.

> "People have more options than they think they do. But most people spend more time planning their vacation than thinking about what they want to do with their lives."
> — Bob McDonald

Contrary to what seems to be popular belief, ignorance is not bliss. Ignorance is pain. And avoiding a problem will not make it disappear. If you'd like to relieve your money pressures, pay off all of your debt, build your nest egg and create financial abundance, then start by making the following suggestions a top priority in your life:

- As soon as you are done reading this chapter, go to your spouse and set a day and time (within the next 7 days) for the two of you to get together to discuss your finances.

- Determine exactly where you are—how much you owe and to whom.

- Sit down together and lay it all out on the table. Don't place blame or get upset with each other. You're a team, a partnership, and together you'll get through this.

- Decide together what you will and will not spend money on. Jointly set your financial goals, put together a plan that will get you there and then work your plan.

- Look at and talk about your plan and how you're doing at least once a week. Then make the necessary adjustments to ensure that you stay on track.

- Be patient, persistent and never give up until you have reached your goals.

This isn't an exercise reserved only for those who are experiencing money pressures. Financially successful couples talk about money and look at their spending and investing habits regularly. Benjamin Franklin once said, *"The secret of success is constancy to purpose."* You have to look at your goals and your progress often, because it's so easy to stray off course.

Identifying and adjusting the thoughts, attitudes and beliefs that you have about money and openly discussing your finances together as a couple will go a long way toward eliminating your money pressures and improving the quality of your marriage.

≈ ∽ ≈

CHAPTER 7

Be Liberal with Your Praise, Compliments and Encouragment

"A kind word is like a Spring day."
— Russian proverb

Several years ago we attended a conference hosted by one of America's most influential public speakers. The conference included a breakout training session for public speaking. Everyone was invited to attend even if they weren't taking part in the training. We went as spectators and what we witnessed left a lasting impression on us.

Before the training started and before the first student gave his presentation, everyone in the audience was given very simple instructions—all feedback was to be positive. We could only tell the presenter what we liked about his or her speech, not what we didn't like or what we thought could be improved.

After the first speaker was finished, the instructors asked for the audience's feedback. The first person started to offer "constructive criticism" and was quickly cut short by one of the instructors and reminded of the feedback rules. The second person to give feedback gave a quick compliment and then started to offer a "suggestion." That too was cut short causing this second person to continue pointing out what they liked about the presentation and the speaker.

It took a little while for the audience to catch on. We are so programmed to point out the negatives, even when our intentions are good. After a while, the compliments and praise from the audience started to flow without hesitation. And the look on the speaker's face when receiving such praise was a sight to see. You could see their confidence level being lifted. They were built up and encouraged.

Speaker after speaker was treated in the same positive manner. The comments weren't vague or general, but rather very specific. Comments like:

- "I love the sound of your voice, I could listen to you for hours."

- "Great job! Your enthusiasm is contagious."

- "You are one sharp dressed person."

- "Something about you evokes trust. I believe you and want to hear what you have to say."

- "You have a wonderful smile."

- "You speak with such passion and conviction. You make me want to join your team."

What an emotional experience—it was amazing! It made us want to be one of the speakers.

You may be thinking, "How are they to improve if no one points out their weaknesses?" That is one of the most common misconceptions regarding improvement.

Excellence is achieved more by focusing on and improving your strengths than by focusing on and improving your weaknesses. This concept has been proven through research.

One such experiment was done with athletes. Each contest was taped so that the athletes could view their performance. The first group of athletes was shown all of the things that they did wrong—their weak points. They were instructed to notice all of their mistakes so that they wouldn't repeat them in the upcoming contests. The second group was shown all of the things that they did right—their strong points. They were instructed to notice all of the things they did right so as to repeat them in the upcoming contests.

After repeating this process, it was found that both groups had improved their performance. But the group that focused on their strong points improved by a much greater margin. Focusing on the strong points versus the weak points produced significantly better results.

You may not be an athlete or a public speaker, but the same rules apply to your life as well. Based on the information above, what do you think is the best way to interact with people in order to get the best results?

What would happen to the quality of your relationships if you were to point out every positive you saw in others?

Do you think this practice would make your spouse, children, friends, relatives and acquaintances feel better about themselves? Would giving them more praise and compliments make them feel better about you? And if they feel better about themselves and they feel better about you, do you think that will affect the way they treat you? Yes, yes and double yes.

> "Nothing is ever lost by courtesy. It is the cheapest of pleasures, costs nothing, and conveys much. It pleases him who gives and receives and thus, like mercy, is twice blessed."
> — Erastus Wiman

As an added bonus, praising and complimenting others makes you feel better about yourself as well. And when you feel better about you, you are more likely to give praise to others, which will cause them to treat you differently—and the cycle continues. It's all about cause and effect.

Make the following an everyday occurrence and watch the world around you change for the better:

- When thinking of a kind word of encouragement or a compliment, speak freely. Don't keep it a secret. A thought in your head doesn't do the other person any good—they can't read your mind.

  ➢ "That outfit really looks nice on you."

  ➢ "You did a great job today, I'm really proud of you."

- When finding fault, hold your tongue. Instead of offering "constructive criticism," look for what you like or appreciate and offer praise instead.

- Try and find people doing things right and tell them about it.

  - ➤ "Thank you for always doing the laundry and making sure everyone has something clean to wear."

  - ➤ "I really appreciate how hard you work, I can always count on you."

- Applaud the accomplishments of others.

  - ➤ "Congratulations on your promotion, you deserve it."

- Smile and treat others with kindness, even if they don't deserve it.

- Treat strangers as though they were your friends.

Everything discussed in this chapter is how you should treat yourself as well. Often we are our own worst enemy.

Go out of your way to find your spouse doing something right. Be liberal with your praise and in the giving of compliments. Smile and treat everyone you meet with kindness, because how you treat the world around you has very much to do with how the world treats you.

Encourage Your Partner

One of the best gifts that you can give your partner is to make them feel good about themselves. As mentioned earlier, the side effect of doing this often is that you start to feel better about yourself as well. Complimenting and praising others will lift you up, whereas criticizing and cutting others down will bring you down. Some of the most miserable people in the world are those who are always finding fault in others. Look for the negative and you will find it. Focus on the negative and it becomes your world, your existence. Conversely, if you focus on what is good, honorable, excellent and praiseworthy, then you'll receive peace and goodness in your life.

And a great way to help others feel good about themselves is through encouragement. But often we confuse encouragement with preaching or nagging, or we use encouragement as a way to get people to do what we want them to. We may have good intentions, but encouragement isn't encouragement unless it relates to something of interest to the recipient. Before we explain what encouragement is, let's take a look at a few of examples of what it is not.

1. Encouraging a friend to stop smoking. If your friend has little or no desire to stop smoking, then anything you say to "encourage" him or her to stop is really just preaching or nagging. You may have good intentions, but pointing out all of the negative aspects of smoking and why they should stop will most likely not move them in the right direction. In fact, it may cause them to dig their heels in and become more reluctant to change.

2. Encouraging your wife to lose weight. This again is not encouragement, but rather communicating your opinion to another person. As a matter of fact, this kind of "encouragement" can often be discouraging to the recipient.

3. Encouraging your husband to take out the trash. Encouraging an act or behavior is not the same as encouraging a person.

The kind of encouragement that we are referring to is something that one can never grow tired of receiving. It builds us up, and helps us reach our goals. Webster's dictionary defines *encourage* as "to inspire with courage, spirit, or hope—to spur on, to give help or patronage to." To inspire with courage, to spur on—that's the kind of encouragement that we need more of in this world!

An Encourager Gives You Courage

An encourager is a person with a lot of power. They have the power to change people's lives. We all have within us the potential to do, have and be more than we can ever imagine. Often, what keeps us from moving in the direction of our desires is a lack of courage. Encouragement increases our courage and belief in ourselves. Encouragement inspires us to become all that we can be. It validates our dreams, reduces our fears and gives us permission to do what we know we should do.

An Encourager Spurs You On

An encourager is more of a cheerleader and less of a preacher. An encourager finds out what you want and unwaveringly supports you. An encourager points out your strengths instead of reminding you of your faults.

Take the weight loss example mentioned earlier. One day your spouse tells you that they want to lose weight and that they are thinking about getting a gym membership. Encouragement would sound like this:

"Jim, you can do anything that you set your mind to. You're very focused and are great at handling difficult situations. Losing weight should be no problem for you. I want you to know that I support you and that I would be willing to diet and work out with you if you think that it would help. Don't worry about the cost of the gym membership, we'll find a way to work it into our budget."

The key to being a good encourager is to find out what people want and then inspire them to move in that direction by reminding them of their strengths and offering to help them if possible.

How often do you encourage your spouse? Are you aware of their dreams and aspirations? Do you build them up and cheer them on? Do you point out their strengths and downplay their weaknesses? Do they feel better about themselves and their circumstances after talking with you? Do you inspire and encourage them to reach for new heights?

Everyone loves to be encouraged, but no one likes to be preached at. At best, your encouragement could change the course of someone's life, at the very least it will make someone's day. Either way you will be planting great seeds into your relationships—seeds that will one day grow to bless your life in ways that you can only imagine. Become an encourager and watch your world become a much brighter place.

⋙ ⊙ ⋘

CHAPTER 8

REMOVE SELFISHNESS FROM YOUR MARRIAGE

"There ain't nothing but one thing wrong
with every one of us, and that's selfishness."
— Will Rogers

L et's face it—we're all selfish by nature. We want
things the way we want them and when we don't
get what we want we can take on any number of
negative attitudes. Sometimes we take it in stride and
continue on with life knowing that life doesn't always bend
to suit our desires. Other times our attitude isn't as honorable.
We may become upset, disappointed, frustrated, even angry.

We may consider ourselves to be mature adults, but
sometimes when we don't get what we want when we want
it, we can act just like children. We complain, clam up
(otherwise know as the silent treatment), pout, whine, yell
and think that life is so unfair. We resist taking personal

responsibility when problems arise in our lives and place the blame on other people or circumstances.

And the marriage relationship is certainly no exception to this general rule.

We often place unreasonably high demands on our spouse, expecting them to complete us or make us happy. We want our partner to act a certain way and do things the way we want them to be done and when they don't, we are quick to point out the error of their ways.

We want to harvest where we haven't planted and take when we haven't given. Sure, we'll give for a while, but if and when we don't receive what we want in return, we withdraw either emotionally or physically or both. We may even try to punish or manipulate our spouse by giving them the silent treatment, nagging or making threats.

Selfishness is poison to a marriage. It can kill intimacy and rob you of the joy that you might otherwise have. And it can keep you from appreciating and enjoying your spouse for who they are.

Not too long ago a lady from Nova Scotia, Canada gave us permission to use her personal story, which is an excellent demonstration of what can happen when we strive to eliminate selfishness from our marriage:

> "What an exciting book this was! Although my husband and I were well on the way to improving our relationship, I found new inspiration by reading *The 21 Day Marriage Makeover*. It helped me rid myself from the last drops of selfishness, lose my defenses and bring our friendship up a notch.
>
> My husband has a weird hobby and despite [the fact] that he does lots for the family, I couldn't forgive him for taking off for a couple months every year to

do what he enjoys. I was allowing myself to be influenced by people's comments that they wouldn't be able to cope with such a thing and that I'm being taken advantage of and that they would not allow this to happen to them.

Despite his numerous invitations to join him, all I wanted was to see him give it up. I was tolerating his hobby, but I was not happy and I did not miss nagging at my husband about it.

The 21 Day Marriage Makeover helped me openly voice and discuss this without being confrontational. We were able to share concerns, information and set our new goals without the usual (though benign) arguing.

I have never felt so close to my husband before.

I'm now able to appreciate my husband for who he is and not for who I wish he was. I now feel the freedom of enjoying MY OWN family life without comparing with other friends and family. By transmitting this message to my husband, I made him feel more loved and trusted. In return, he is more open to me than ever before.

Belief, knowledge and their application can be so powerful. I can only say THANK YOU to Darren and Donna for writing this book. I am sure it is going to help millions of people as it helped me."

— Maria P.

"Life is not always what one wants it to be,
but to make the best of it, as it is,
is the only way of being happy."
— Jennie Jerome Churchill

Sometimes we have every right to be disappointed or get mad and give our spouse a piece of our mind. But that doesn't mean that we have to exercise that right. Sometimes overlooking a wrong and choosing to be patient, forgiving and loving is one of the most unselfish things that we can do.

To argue and fight every time something negative happens is to treat your marriage like a battleground and your spouse like the enemy. Attacking your partner (even if they are to blame) whether aggressively or passive aggressively isn't going to improve the quality of your relationship. But choosing to make the best of a negative situation will.

> "I find that it is not circumstances in which we are placed, but the spirit in which we face them, that constitutes our comfort."
> — Elizabeth T. King

The following story sent to us by a dear friend demonstrates that we can't always control what happens to us, but we *can* control how we react to what happens to us:

> "Last night when I came home at 9:30 pm the baby was still up and the house was a mess. I was quite irritated. We had to get up early in the morning and had a full day ahead of ourselves. I thought I could either get really mad and blow my stack or I could take this as an opportunity to give the baby a bath. I opted for the latter and found myself not being angry at my husband. I had a choice to make and I chose to not let it bother me and the end result was a harmonious night."

Personal Evaluation:

1. When you feel that your relationship is getting off track and you aren't as happy as you would like to be, do you:

    a. *think of all of the things that your spouse could do differently in order to make you happy, thus improving the quality of your marriage, or*

    b. *do you think of the things that you can do differently to make your spouse happy, thus improving the quality of your marriage?*

2. Do you get upset when your partner doesn't give you something special on your birthday, anniversary, Valentines Day, Sweetest Day, Mother's Day, Father's Day, Christmas, etc.?

    a. *yes*

    b. *no*

3. What thoughts occupy your mind the most:

    a. *all of the things that you wish that your spouse would do for you, or*

    b. *all of the things that you want to do for your spouse?*

4. Do you nag, complain, pout and/or whine when things don't go the way you would like them to?

    a. *yes*

    b. *no*

5. Do you derive more pleasure from:

    a. *being served by your mate, or*

    b. *serving your mate?*

6. Do you:

    a. *fantasize about what it would be like to be with someone else, or*

    b. *think about all of the things that you love about your partner?*

7. Do you:

    a. *hold grudges and bring up the past especially in the heat of an argument, or*

    b. *are you quick to forgive and leave the past in the past?*

8. When hurt or angry, do you try and punish your spouse by withholding affection, communication or sex?

    a. *yes*

    b. *no*

9. When you argue about money:

    a. *do you play the blame game, or*

    b. *is it a "family" problem where you both take equal responsibility?*

10. Do you view marriage as:

    a. *each person for themselves, or*

    b. *a team sport where if you hurt or help your partner you are actually hurting or helping yourself?*

11. Do you:

   a. *squelch your partner's ideas and tell them to be "realistic" or do you give your goals a higher priority, or*

   b. *do you support and encourage your spouse to discover and pursue their dreams?*

If you answered "b" on 8 or more of the above questions, then you're probably in pretty good shape. If not, then there is definitely room for improvement.

Robert J. McCracken observed that, *"The most infectiously joyous men and women are those who forget themselves in thinking about others and serving others."* A happy marriage is filled with acts of love. Go out of your way to serve your spouse and to give him or her love in the way that he or she needs love. Continually praise, encourage and lift them up. Focus on their good points and forgive their mistakes.

To love is to please and to love much is to please often. True love is the opposite of selfishness.

CHAPTER 9

INVEST "QUANTITY" TIME

"One of the great illusions of our time is
that love is self-sustaining. It is not. Love
must be fed and nurtured, contstantly renewed.
That demands ingenuity and consideration,
but first and foremost, it demands time."
—David Mace

Most of us need to look at time differently. We
can start by changing the words we use to
describe it. All too often we use the phrase "spend
time" when we really mean, "invest time." You *spend* time
mowing the lawn. You *invest* time with your spouse.

When you *spend* something, there is a cost. This cost is
called an opportunity cost. Time's opportunity cost is what
you have to give up because you chose to spend time doing
something else. If you spend one hour mowing the lawn,
you gave up the opportunity to wash the car during that
time.

Investing is a completely different animal. You invest

with the intention of receiving more in return than what you originally invested.

We're all familiar with investing money. You invest $100 in a mutual fund at nine percent annual return and you end up with $109 at the end of the year. Investing time works in a similar fashion, although the return on investment isn't always easily measured or predicted.

> "An unhurried sense of time
> is in itself a form of wealth."
> — Bonnie Friedman

Time with your spouse should be considered investment time. Invest as much time in your relationship as you can. Believe that you will receive a great return on your investment, because you will. If you think of this time as an opportunity cost (I could be doing this or that right now) then your time is spent and you will not receive as profitable a return, if any.

In our busy society there's a lot of talk about quality time versus quantity time. In most cases, this is our way of justifying not doing the things that we should be doing. If you are *spending* time, then quality-focused time is very important.

If you're *investing* time, why would you want to sell yourself short by only investing a little? If your definition of quality time is being there in the moment or that your mind is not wandering or thinking about other things, then we agree that quality time is very important.

If quality time is your way of making yourself feel better for only spending half an hour talking with your mate on Tuesday evening because other things took a higher priority, then quality time should be eliminated from your vocabulary.

You can't rush your relationship-building experience. Time is very important even if it is just sitting next to each other holding hands and not saying a word. From now on, think of quantity time as being a key ingredient in building a relationship that will stand the test of time.

CHAPTER 10

REALIZE THAT FLAWED DOESN'T MEAN BAD

"A good garden may have some weeds."
— Thomas Fuller

One of the most sought after and prized substances in the world are diamonds. Songs have been written about them and movies titled after them. They are the focal point of many engagement and wedding rings and anniversary presents.

A diamond can symbolize love and appreciation. It can also be a status symbol, signify the passing of a milestone or award accomplishment. Diamonds can add beauty and brilliance to an otherwise plain looking piece of jewelry.

Of all of the things a diamond is there is one thing that it's not. For the most part a diamond isn't perfect—it's flawed. Sure there are flawless diamonds, but very few people own them because they are rare and extremely expensive.

Yet the fact that almost every diamond is flawed doesn't make them bad, worthless or undesirable. As a matter of fact, a man-made diamond is virtually perfect in every way, void of inclusions and unwanted color, yet they are almost free when compared to the real thing.

> "If you're looking for perfection,
> look in the mirror. If you find it
> there, expect it elsewhere."
> — Malcolm Forbes

Why is it that we so readily accept a flawed diamond, giving it great value, yet we look at our own imperfections or the imperfections of others as unacceptable?

We can tolerate the fact that our diamond has some carbon in it or is slightly yellow, but when our friends, loved ones or spouse does something wrong or doesn't live up to our expectations we get offended, hurt, disappointed or angry. Why are we so quick to judge and so slow to forgive?

> "Friendships aren't perfect, and yet they
> are very precious. For me, not expecting
> perfection all in one place was a great release."
> — Letty Cottin Pogrebin

We are all flawed, but these flaws, like the flaws in a diamond, don't make us worthless or undesirable. They make us human. If you strive for perfection, you will never measure up. If you expect it in others, they will always let you down. Instead, you should strive for excellence, doing your best, and look for the good in others as well.

> *"Use what talents you have; the woods*
> *would have little music if no birds sang*
> *their song except those who sang best."*
> — Reverend Oliver G. Wilson

Like a diamond, you don't have to be perfect to be of great value. You can demonstrate excellence while still having flaws. You can make a difference even though you make mistakes.

You don't have to be good looking to be attractive, have a lot of money in order to be rich or possess great knowledge in order to positively impact someone's life.

> *"Have patience with all things, but chiefly have*
> *patience with yourself. Do not lose courage*
> *in considering your own imperfections,*
> *but instantly set about remedying them—*
> *every day begin the task anew."*
> — Saint Francis de Sales

Unlike a diamond, we have the ability to improve ourselves—not to be perfect or to be like someone else, but to be a better version of ourselves.

> *"Always be a first-rate version of yourself, instead of*
> *a second-rate version of somebody else."*
> —Judy Garland

To strive for personal excellence may seem to be selfish or self-centered, but it isn't. It is actually one of the most unselfish things that you can do because as you grow as a person you begin to treat others better and have a more positive impact on your environment.

The next time you start to get down on yourself or your spouse, stop focusing on the flaws and start looking at the sparkle. You don't continually curse the flaws in your diamond. Then why do so with yourself or with others?

Don't allow past mistakes or personal limitations to rob you of becoming the person you were meant to be. And don't let the flaws that you see in others keep you from experiencing awesome relationships.

> "Rebellion against your handicaps gets you nowhere. Self-pity gets you nowhere. One must have the adventurous daring to accept oneself as a bundle of possibilities and undertake the most interesting game in the world—making the most of one's best."
> — Harry Emerson Fosdick

We are all flawed human beings, but it isn't our flaws that matter most, but rather what we do with what we have. What will you do today?

CHAPTER 11

Master the Art of Conflict Resolution

"What counts in making a happy marriage
is not so much how compatible you are, but
how you deal with incompatibility."
— George Levinger

O bviously, healthy on-going communication between
you and your spouse is absolutely necessary in
order for the two of you to grow closer together
versus drifting further apart. But what many couples don't
realize is the fact that not everyone communicates in the same
way.

Odds are pretty good that you and your partner have
very different communication styles. It is very important that
you recognize, appreciate and learn how to best deal with
these differences. One difference that you may have in your
relationship is how each of you handles confrontation,
conflict or strong emotions.

People usually fall into one of two camps. Their initial reaction is either fight or flight. They either want to address the issue head on usually expressing strong emotion or they want to avoid it at all costs.

As with our many other differences, don't think of one type as right and the other as wrong. They are just different. Both can be potentially harmful reactions if not handled properly. Continual fighting can be damaging to your relationship and so can avoiding issues that need to be addressed.

The following is a brief story taken from Chapter 7 of our marriage improvement program *The 21 Day Marriage Makeover* entitled *Discover Who You Are and Who Your Spouse Is*, which describes one reason why these differences occur:

The differences in our upbringing

We all grew up in different surroundings, in different homes, and with different parents. These environmental factors played a major role in forming who we are today. Many of the conflicts that arise among couples can be traced back to the way in which they grew up. The following story demonstrates how our childhood can affect our marriages.

Sally and John—fight or flight

Sally was raised to never yell at someone or lose her temper. Whenever her parents' discussions would get too heated, they would drop the conversation, give each other some space and time to cool off and then proceed in a calm manner at a later time. The absolute worst thing that one could do would be to yell at the other person. That would be extremely disrespectful.

John, on the other hand, came from a very expressive household. Everyone said what was on his or her mind and expressed his or her feelings with great emotion. Holding back one's feelings was a sign of mistrust. Heated discussions were the norm, and it was a sign of great disrespect if someone would walk out in the middle of a conversation (fight).

Sally and John fell in love and got married. Sally loves John's passion and John appreciates Sally's even-mannered calmness. The first time they get into an argument, however, John raises his voice and Sally, sensing that things could get out of hand, walks out of the room. This makes John even more upset, and he follows her speaking even louder. She knows that they need time to cool off and he knows that they need to talk things through. They both get frustrated and can't figure out why their spouse acts the way that he or she does.

This kind of problem can exist and cause frustration in a marriage for years, possibly even for the length of the marriage. One of the primary reasons that a conflict like this can continue for years is because we ask the wrong questions and come up with the wrong answers. We forget to put on our private investigator's hat and discover what it is that causes our spouse to act and react the way that he or she does.

John may think that Sally is always trying to avoid confrontation and would rather ignore their problems than openly discuss them. Sally may feel that John doesn't care about her feelings because he is so quick to yell at her and get into a fight. The real reason for their conflict may be as simple as the way that each of them defines respect. Sally feels that it's disrespectful to yell at the people you love and care about, and John feels that it's disrespectful to walk out on a discussion with the people that you love and care about.

Often these differences fall along gender lines where men tend to have a greater difficulty handling conflict and flee, whereas women fight. These men may not flee physically, but they can disengage emotionally bringing an end to the communication leading to marital dissatisfaction for both parties.

No combination is ideal however. Two fighters can create an explosive relationship, one that may send one of the participants packing. Two avoiders often live in a world of unresolved issues and suppressed emotions. The emotions are still there and can erupt at any time or even destroy the sense of intimacy between them. A fighter and an avoider may cause each other to feel misunderstood, unappreciated, frustrated, resentful and insecure in their relationship.

It's important that both the fighter and the avoider recognize that conflict in a relationship is nothing more than an opportunity for growth. Unresolved issues cause you to grow apart while resolved issues cause you to grow stronger together.

According to Dr. Florence Kaslow, clinical professor at Duke University in Durham, NC, the major factor contributing to satisfaction in couples is joint problem-solving ability. Dr. Howard Markman, head of the Center for Marital and Family Studies at the University of Denver, states, *"Rather than viewing differences and conflicts as a sign of incompatibility, couples need to see them as opportunities for developing skills that they can use for the rest of their relationship."* Dr. Markman has found that *"Thirty to fifty percent of couples are mutually abusive—now that's a sign of poor conflict management. Abuse erupts from frustration of not being able to manage negative feelings."*

The Fighter

You have the tendency to react quickly and with great emotion. You want to be heard and understood and you want it now. When it comes to communication, you don't like loose ends or unfinished business. You speak with emotion and conviction and usually raise your voice when doing so.

It may be best for you to distance yourself from the event prior to engaging your spouse. Give yourself a little time to cool down, collect your thoughts and reflect on the situation. Think about how you can communicate your thoughts so that you don't appear to be attacking your spouse.

When your spouse approaches you about an issue, remain calm, listen and don't become defensive or try to turn the conversation around by bringing up all of the things that they do wrong. Your spouse's feelings are their feelings. Arguing or telling them that they shouldn't feel that way won't make things better.

Also, make sure to watch your spouse's body language when expressing your feelings. If they avoid eye contact, stiffen up or don't respond, you may have lost them emotionally. You may think that everything is okay because you have vented and gotten your feelings off your chest, however, things may be far from okay. You may feel better, but your partner may feel worse—a lot worse.

The Avoider

You can't stand conflict. Just the thought of it can make your heart race and your palms sweat. You would rather walk away and/or suppress your emotions than engage in a potentially heated discussion. When your spouse engages you, you either avoid the conflict or shut down emotionally.

You are afraid that expressing your feelings will make things worse between you and your mate. When in fact, this avoidance and suppression of feelings will only make matters worse. Your continual avoidance or flight response may eventually cause your spouse to withdraw as well. This can turn soul mates into roommates and destroy intimacy.

Know that the only way to resolve problems is to face them and deal with them.

Don't be afraid to confront your spouse. It may be uncomfortable, but so is living with unresolved issues. When your spouse shares his or her feelings or becomes confrontational, don't walk away or shut down, but try to understand that even though it may seem like a personal attack, what they're really attacking is the action not you.

The differences between the sexes and in our talents, skills, abilities, personalities and upbringing make life exciting. You can choose to become frustrated by these differences or you can recognize them as being part of what makes us who we are.

For you to understand your spouse and for him or her to understand you is not about figuring out *why* they are different, but rather to discover *what* these differences are and then learn to appreciate and live with them.

And remember, the health of any long-term relationship is not so much dependent upon how compatible you are, but rather how you deal with your incompatibilities.

The 11 Rules of Engagement

"Many marriages would be better if the husband and the wife clearly understood that they are on the same side."
— Zig Ziglar

In any relationship there are bound to be disagreements and arguments, and a marriage is no exception. Disagreements are healthy, they can cause you to take a look at things from someone else's perspective. If you are open minded and willing to hear the other person's point of view and willing to consider a different way of thinking, a disagreement can lead to a great outcome. Better in fact than the outcome you would have experienced had the disagreement not taken place.

"Honest differences are often a healthy sign of progress."
— Mahatma Gandhi

This dynamic is know as synergy. Synergy is derived from the Greek word *synergos*, which means "working together." We have all heard the saying that two heads are better than one. Synergism suggests that two people working together toward a common goal are much more effective than the combined efforts of those two people working separately. Through synergy, one plus one doesn't equal two, it equals three, five or even twenty.

The key words being "working together." If the purpose of the disagreement is to prove yourself right and the other person wrong, then synergy cannot take place and the disagreement will serve no positive purpose whatsoever. In fact, a disagreement entered into with this intention will only strain the relationship and make matters worse.

Now let's talk about a more serious matter—arguments and fights. Arguments, like disagreements, can be healthy to a relationship. That is as long as certain rules of engagement are practiced.

The 11 Rules of Engagement are as follows:

1. Give yourself some time to cool down and collect your thoughts.

2. Choose the right time.

3. Offer reassurance.

4. Seek first to understand before being understood.

5. Know that it's okay to disagree.

6. Don't bring up the past.

7. Avoid statements like "you always" and "you never."

8. Talk about the "behavior" not the "person."

9. Avoid name calling, criticism, sarcasm and put-downs.

10. When given the chance to be right or to be kind, choose kind.

11. Don't go to bed angry.

"Never yell at each other
unless the house is on fire."
— H. Jackson Brown, Jr.

Before we give a brief explanation of these rules, we feel it necessary to address the topic of fighting. A fight is simply an argument that got out of control. While disagreements and arguments can be a healthy part of a relationship, fighting is not. A fight always leaves one person or both feeling worse about you, themselves and/or the relationship. Fighting should be avoided at all costs.

And if your partner insists on fighting, you have the choice not to participate. It takes two to tango and you can decide to remain calm in every situation.

Now let's take a closer look at *The 11 Rules of Engagement*.

1. Give yourself some time to cool down and collect your thoughts. In the heat of the moment it's easy to say things that we don't really mean, to blow things out of proportion, to overreact or to say mean and hurtful things. When our emotions are the strongest that is when we need to practice the discipline of calming ourselves down, taking slow deep breaths and giving ourselves a little time to reflect on the situation.

"When angry, count to ten before you speak;
if very angry, an hundred."
— Thomas Jefferson

The first thing to do is to decide if what just happened is really worth getting yourself all worked up about. J. Kenfield Morley observed that *"Man is measured by the size of the thing that makes him angry."* If you get mad, sad, hurt or offended often or by the smallest things, that's not a reflection of the person that you think made you feel that way—it's a reflection of your personal growth. It says that you're willing to allow other people and circumstances to have control over your emotions.

> "Every moment that you spend upset,
> in despair, in anguish, angry or hurt because of the
> behavior of anybody else in your life, is a moment
> in which you have given up control of your life."
> — Dr. Wayne W. Dyer

So when your emotions are high, give yourself some time for honest reflection.

2. Choose the right time. There is a time and place for everything. Before you express your strong emotions or engage in what could become a heated discussion, make sure the timing is right.

Entering into such a discussion at the mall, a friend's house, in front of your kids or while your mate is in the middle of doing something, is not a good idea. You need your privacy and you need your mate's full attention. If necessary, schedule a time for the two of you to talk.

3. Offer reassurance. After you have both agreed to the right time and place for your discussion, tell your spouse that you love them and that your relationship means a lot to you.

Let them know that you appreciate the fact that they are willing to listen to your feelings. When it's time for your conversation, reassure them again.

4. Seek first to understand before being understood.
Everyone wants to be heard, to be understood. And few things make someone feel better about you than when you listen to them intently, when you empathize with them. Knowing this gives you great power in any discussion or argument.

> "The reason why we have two ears
> and only one mouth is that we may
> listen the more and talk the less."
> — Zeno of Citium

Before stating your case, let the other person share their view. Let them talk until they are done talking. Repeat back some of the things that they said in your own words so that you're sure that you understood exactly what they meant. Once they have shared their concerns and feel like they've been heard, then it is your turn to speak.

> "If you will invest time in listening,
> you will save that time in arguments."
> — Joyce Meyer

By doing this you will have effectively diffused a potential argument, brought his or her defenses down and set the stage for you to be heard. By talking first, your words may just fall on deaf ears.

5. Know that it's okay to disagree. As mentioned earlier, disagreements can be very healthy in a relationship. Disagreements can also be very damaging if we have the need to always be right and if we view opinions that differ from our own as being wrong.

Many couples don't realize that it's perfectly acceptable to agree to disagree. One person doesn't have to be right and the other wrong. It's possible for you to have different opinions and both be right.

In order for one to accept this kind of disagreement, he or she must not take it personally. Too often we take these disagreements or differences of opinion as a personal rejection. We forget that our spouse is rejecting our idea, not us. It's important that you see the difference.

A waitress at a café goes from table to table asking people if they would like a cup of coffee. The first person she approaches says no. The second does as well. The third person that she asks also rejects the offer.

Does the waitress try to talk the customers into trying a cup? Does she take the rejection personally, thinking that they must not like her or that she is doing something wrong? Does she get mad at people because they don't want or like coffee? Does she think that there is something wrong with them because they don't want any coffee?

Accept the fact that you and your partner will disagree about many things. How you handle these disagreements will determine your peace of mind and the health of your relationship.

6. Don't bring up the past. Stay on the topic at hand and leave the past in the past where it belongs. If you feel the need to bring up the past, it may mean that you've never let it go and are still holding on to bitterness or unforgiveness. If so, let it go and put it behind you because bitterness and unforgiveness hurts the person holding on to it and it will also hurt your relationship.

Bringing up the past could also mean that you feel like you're losing the argument. In a relationship if there is a winner and a loser, you both end up losing. Your goal shouldn't be to win. Your goal should be to resolve the issue in a way that makes you both feel good about each other and the relationship.

7. Avoid statements like "you always" and "you never". Statements like these do nothing more than make people want to defend themselves and there's little hope that anything that you say afterward will be heard or accepted. Remember, your goal is to improve the relationship, not make the other person feel bad.

8. Talk about the "behavior" not the "person". Don't say "you make me so angry" or "you hurt my feelings." Instead say, "When you weren't willing to listen to me this morning, that really hurt my feelings." That way you're telling your partner that you don't like or accept the behavior not that you don't like or accept him or her.

9. Avoid name calling, criticism, sarcasm and put-downs. Not only are these things immature and damaging to your relationship, but according to research recently reported in USA Today, they are also bad for your health. According to this report, couples whose disagreements were peppered with criticism, sarcasm and put-downs took 40 percent longer to heal from wounds. These "hostile" couples were also found to have poorer immune functions, more respiratory infections, higher blood pressure and greater difficulty coping with stressful jobs.

> "The pleasure of criticizing robs us
> of the pleasure of being moved
> by some very fine things."
> — Jean De La Bruyère

10. When given the chance to be right or to be kind, choose kind. This advice will transform your life and give you a sense of peace like few things can. It's incredibly liberating when you no longer feel the need to be right. Try it out for yourself for seven consecutive days and see the positive impact it will have on your relationships.

> *"Do you want to be right or do you want to be happy?"*
> — Brian Tracy

11. Don't go to bed angry. At times it's very difficult, almost impossible, not to get angry. But to hold on to that anger is a choice. You may not be able to resolve all of your arguments before the sun goes down, but you can decide not to go to bed angry.

Consistently adhere to these 11 Rules of Engagement and you'll see the quality of your relationships transform before your very eyes.

A healthy marriage is not defined by being problem- or conflict-free, but rather by resolving your problems and conflicts in a way that makes you both feel understood and secure in your relationship.

Treat your spouse with kindness and always be on the lookout for ways to improve your relationship.

CHAPTER 12

EMBRACE THE HEALING POWER OF FORGIVENESS

"To err is human; to forgive, divine."
— Alexander Pope

Unforgiveness can destroy any relationship and a marriage is no exception. It can also destroy the person who holds on to it. Studies have shown that unforgiveness can even make you sick. Unforgiveness can lead to resentment, anger, bitterness and cynicism. How can you have an awesome relationship with someone that you are bitter toward?

"Bitterness imprisons life; love releases it."
— Harry Emerson Fosdick

There's another very important side to forgiveness within a relationship. And that's to ask for forgiveness. Depending on one's personality, this can be even harder than forgiving. This is where pride pokes its ugly head into the picture. Why should you ask for forgiveness when you were right and your actions or words were justified?

Marriage is not a contest. What difference does it make who is right and who is wrong if an action or words are coming between you and the one you love?

The phrase "love is never having to say you're sorry," must have been coined by a divorce attorney. If you never apologize, then your marriage may end in divorce.

> "The forgiving state of mind is a
> magnetic power for attracting good."
> — Catherine Ponder

Success in any area of life requires a lot of work and marriage is no exception. Be sensitive enough to know when something is bothering your spouse. Ask if you have done something to offend or hurt them. If so, tell them that you are sorry. If you are on the receiving end, accept their apology and forget about it.

> "To be wronged is nothing
> unless you continue to remember it."
> — Confucius

Forgive and forget. Is that possible? We get concerned when we hear someone bring up something that someone did to offend them several years ago. Is it just that they have a good memory? We don't think so. It is more likely that they never forgave that person. Some people even try to use past events as leverage against the other person. Again, a marriage is not a competition. In a marriage, if there is a winner and a loser, then you both lose.

> " 'I can forgive, but I cannot forget' is only
> another way of saying, 'I will not forgive.'
> Forgiveness ought to be like a canceled
> note—torn in two and burned up so that
> it never can be shown against one."
> — Henry Ward Beecher

Unforgiveness can also be a trap that you don't want to get out of. You may think that you are punishing the person that you have unforgiveness toward. Deep down you are saying, "You really hurt me and I'm going to punish you by never forgiving you for what you have done." If you do that, whom are you really punishing? Is the person who hurt you affected by the feelings that you hold inside? Of course not—they will go on with their life, while this unforgiveness eats away at you.

> "To carry a grudge is like being
> stung to death by one bee."
> — William H. Walton

By not forgiving someone, you give them the power to hurt you over and over again every time that you think about them or the situation. Do you want that person to have that much control over you? Do you want them to control your life, your health and your marriage? If your answer is no, then forgive them because unforgiveness only hurts the person holding it.

You may also feel that forgiving someone makes what they did to you okay. Forgiveness is not acceptance. Just because you forgive someone doesn't mean that what they did was right or that it is okay for them to do it again.

We can't always control what happens to us, but we can control how we react to those events. We can decide how we will let those events affect the rest of our life. Forgive, let it go, and let the healing begin in your life.

Self-forgiveness

There is another form of unforgiveness that isn't as obvious as that held against another. This type of unforgiveness is the unforgiveness that you have toward yourself.

It isn't always as emotional or intense as the unforgiveness held against another yet it can still have an enormous impact on your life. We believe that most people who hold this kind of unforgiveness don't even know that they do.

We have all done and said things that we wish we hadn't. We all make mistakes both big and small. To live a flawless life is impossible.

If you have wronged someone, ask for forgiveness and then forgive yourself. If the person is no longer living or if you have no idea where they live or how to contact them, write them a letter asking for their forgiveness. When you are finished with the letter, say "I'm sorry, please forgive me" out loud and then shred or burn the letter. It's finished, you can now let it go.

Perhaps you beat yourself up over missed opportunities, recent or past failures, not following your gut feelings, procrastination, laziness, etc. If you are participating in this thing called life, then you have plenty of opportunities to get upset with yourself.

There is nothing wrong with getting mad, it often causes us to improve our life and the world around us, but don't hold on to this anger, let it go. Don't resent yourself for making mistakes; just try your best not to repeat them.

No matter what you have done or what has happened to you, it's okay to forgive yourself and start all over. Each new day brings us the opportunity to more wisely start over again. We can't change our past; however, letting go of the past is one way to ensure a brighter tomorrow.

> "When I look at the future,
> it's so bright, it burns my eyes."
> — Oprah Winfrey

Forgive others and forgive yourself. Set yourself free from resentful thoughts so that you can find peace and live a more abundant life.

CHAPTER 13

QUIT
KEEPING
SCORE

"In marriage, each partner is to be an
encourager rather than a critic, a forgiver
rather than a collector of hurts, an
enabler rather than a reformer."
— H. Norman Wright and Gary J. Oliver

When playing basketball, a round of golf, tennis or any other sport, keeping score can be fun. A little friendly competition keeps us on our toes and causes us to try a little harder than we otherwise would. Card and board games also have scoring methods so that we know who's winning and what it will take for the other players to catch up.

If done with the right attitude, keeping score while playing games or participating in sports is relatively harmless. Keeping score in a relationship, however, prevents growth, weakens communication and will most certainly cause ongoing frustration.

Don't Lose That Lovin' Feeling

If you want to lose the loving feelings that you have toward your spouse, just focus on all of the things that you do for your relationship/family and all of the things that your mate doesn't do. You may never have realized it before, but every time your mind drifts toward this kind of thinking, you are keeping score. In your mind you are keeping track of all that you do and all that your partner doesn't do.

> "What we see depends mainly
> on what we look for."
> — John Lubbock

When keeping score, there is a winner and there is a loser and unfortunately "you" come out the loser. This can make you feel taken advantage of and cause you to become resentful. And because what you focus on the most expands and becomes more real, all of a sudden your spouse's innocent request, "Hey, could you pick up a loaf of bread on your way home?" becomes another mark against them on your scorecard.

> "We are not troubled by things, but by
> the opinion which we have of things."
> — Epictetus

Even if you never share these thoughts with your spouse, your mental "scorecard" will adversely affect your relationship. That's because thoughts aren't just innocent harmless things. Thoughts are the foundation upon which everything is built. Positive or empowering thoughts lead to positive results, whereas negative or disempowering thoughts lead to negative results.

> "Our best friends and our worst enemies
> are our thoughts. A thought can do more good
> than a doctor or a banker or a faithful friend.
> It can also do us more harm than a brick."
> — Dr. Frank Crane

It won't take long at all before these negative thoughts about your spouse turn into negative comments or actions toward them. This in turn causes your mate to become defensive or makes them feel unappreciated for all of the things that they do. And the downward relationship spiral begins, where one negative thing leads to another.

"The Relationship Cycle"

Your thoughts about your spouse = how you feel about him or her = how you treat your partner = how your partner feels about you = how your partner treats you = how you treat each other = the quality of your marriage.

You Have a Choice

It is almost impossible to be extremely grateful that you have been blessed with a wonderful spouse and at the same time be upset about all of the things that he or she does (or doesn't do) to upset you. Our minds are not very good at focusing on two different things at the same time. Therefore, you have the choice—you can either choose to focus on the negatives or you can choose to be thankful for the positives. Which choice do you think will improve the quality of your marriage?

"The unthankful heart...discovers no
mercies; but the thankful heart...will find,
in every hour, some heavenly blessings."
— Henry Ward Beecher

Keeping Score Is Nothing More Than a Bad Habit

The next time you catch your thoughts about your spouse drifting toward the negative, get rid of those negative thoughts and replace them with positive ones. Think about all of the things that your partner does for you and your family. Focus on what you like about him or her.

Controlling your thoughts isn't easy, but it can be done. You may have had these negative mental habits for a long time. So it will take time to reverse these habits. Not only will it take time, but it will also take consistency. You have to constantly fill your mind with positive thoughts in order to overshadow the negative ones. Our mind is like a computer, and we need to reprogram it. Repetition is a way that we can rewrite our programming.

Also, make sure not to keep score of past wrongs. This will keep you from throwing your scorecard in your spouse's face in the event of an argument, which will of course only make matters worse.

Keeping track of past wrongs is nothing more than harbored unforgiveness. And unforgiveness can poison your relationship, destroy your personal peace and limit your happiness.

"Forgiveness means
letting go of the past."
— Gerald Jampolsky

If you're going to keep score, make a list of all of the things that you like about your partner. Then go to your spouse and show them your scorecard. That's how you create a winning team!

CHAPTER 14

STOP LIVING WITH REGRET

"If only. Those must be the two
saddest words in the world."
— Mercedes Lackey

Is there anything about your life that you regret? If you are like most people, you have a long list of things that you wish you hadn't done and an even longer list of things that you wish you would've done. Anyone who has reflected back on their life has felt regret to one degree or another, but is regret an emotion that serves you or hinders you?

The kind of regret we're talking about here isn't the feeling that you experience when you go grocery shopping at noon on Saturday, stand in the checkout line for a half hour and then wish that you had gone shopping early Friday morning instead. The regret we want to deal with is the kind that stirs up strong negative emotions—the kind that makes you feel bad and wish that you could go back in time and do things differently.

Reflecting on your past so that you can learn from it and make better decisions today is a good thing. Taking an inventory of your life to determine if you're on the right track and living a life of purpose is a necessary thing. But living a life of regret is a waste of time and emotional energy.

Regret, like many other disempowering emotions, causes you to dwell on the negative instead of the positive. This negative focus will in turn attract more negativity into your life, whether it be negative circumstances or more negative emotions. Regret can be a paralytic keeping you from living a full and abundant life and it can also cause you to drown in the sea of self-pity.

> "Self-pity is a death that has no resurrection, a sinkhole from which no rescuing hand can drag you because you have chosen to sink."
> — Elizabeth Elliot

One of the reasons regret can be so harmful is because it never works alone. Regret is not a solo emotion—it's always intermingled with other negative emotions like hurt, bitterness, anger, feelings of loss, sadness, betrayal, dissatisfaction and the like. Another reason is that it causes you to live in the past—a place where you can never revisit and something that you can never change.

Now for the good news...You don't have to live a life of regret. Starting right now, you can live your life where it is supposed to be lived—right here, right now, in the present.

So how do you keep regret from getting the better of you?

1. Change your focus. As mentioned earlier, you can either choose to dwell on the negative things in your life and from your past or you can choose to dwell on the positive. The regrets of yesterday can haunt you only when you choose to focus on them.

2. Forgive. None of us fully understands the awesome liberating and healing power of forgiveness. If we did, we would treat unforgiveness like a hot potato and let go of it as soon as we can. You may wonder what forgiveness has to do with regret. As we stated earlier, many other emotions can be rolled up together with regret, and unforgiveness can be one of them.

Before you can let go of regret, you may need to forgive yourself. We all make mistakes and do things that we wish we hadn't, but continuing to beat yourself up over such things is a form of unforgiveness. It's okay to forgive yourself and let it go.

If your regret is due to something that you said, did or didn't do to someone else, then ask that person for forgiveness.

3. Take action. Several years ago we were talking with a young man who was describing some of the rental properties he had purchased. His brother was also moving away from being an employee and recently purchased an existing business. Their dad was listening in on the conversation and later told us that he wished that he had taken more chances like his boys are.

You could hear the regret in his voice. The sad thing was, his regret was completely unnecessary. He was only about fifty-eight years old and could still do the very things he was regretting. Instead of living with regret, all he needed to do was take action.

Do you regret that you never furthered your education? If so, then sign up for a class or two next semester. Do you regret that you never learned how to paint, dance or learn a musical instrument? If so, then sign up for some lessons *today*. And if you regret that you didn't spend more time with your spouse or kids in the past, take the time and do it now.

Will Durant said *"Forget mistakes. Forget failures. Forget everything except what you're going to do now and do it. Today is your lucky day."* Colonel Sanders was sixty-five years old when he actively began franchising Kentucky Fried Chicken. KFC began with a sixty-five-year-old gentleman who used his $105 Social Security check to start a business.

What regrets do you have that could be eliminated by simply taking action today?

4. Don't use regret as an alibi. As long as you hold on to your regrets, you may think that you have an excuse for why your life isn't the way you would like it to be. It's a lot easier for us to blame ourselves (or others) for what we did or didn't do in the past than it is to take responsibility for our happiness and success in life today.

5. Know that you have a choice. Regardless of what you have or haven't done in the past, know that your future is created by the choices that you make today. It's okay to learn from the past, just don't live there.

> *"You did what you knew how to do, and when you knew better, you did better."*
> — Maya Angelou

The next time you start to think thoughts of regret, simply remind yourself that you made your past decisions based on what you thought was best at the time. We all learn, change and grow throughout our lifetime. Today is a new day filled with endless possibilities. Think about all of the beauty and good fortune in your life and continue to build a future that you can be proud of.

CHAPTER 15

LIKE
YOURSELF

"When you like yourself, the sun seems
a little brighter, the grass a little greener
and life's obstacles a little smaller. The first
step toward enjoying life is to like yourself."
— Darren & Donna McNees

On the surface it would seem that the happiest couples would consist of two people who are madly in love with each other—two people who enjoy each other's company, who really like each other.

Or maybe the most successful marriages consist of two people who serve each other unselfishly, placing the needs and desires of their partner above their own. Perhaps the happiest couples are the ones who handle conflict best, who work as a team to get through all of life's challenges instead of turning on each other by arguing and fighting all the time.

There are several key ingredients that go into creating a wonderful marriage. Many of them are obvious, yet not every couple practices them. Other ingredients are not so well known, yet they have a profound impact on the quality of one's marriage. And some are even overlooked by the most well trained marriage counselors. This chapter will touch on one of those often-overlooked ingredients.

We have found that some of the happiest marriages consist of two people who each like themselves. When you have a healthy self-love, it's easier for you to accept the love of others. When you're at peace with yourself, the world becomes a more peaceful place. When you like yourself, others are more drawn to you, and they feel more comfortable being around you. When you like yourself, you believe that you deserve the best that life has to offer and it is this belief that brings the best into your life.

It's very rare that someone receives more in life than they feel that they deserve. And if they do, they have a hard time enjoying it, or even worse, they will slowly but surely push it out of their life. Some people will even unconsciously sabotage their success.

The following are a few common examples:

- An overweight person goes on a diet and is very successful at losing the first thirty pounds or so. Then out of nowhere, for no particular reason, they go off their diet and gain back even more weight then they had lost.

- A person works very hard to earn and save a fair amount of money and then loses it almost overnight. Or they can strive to get ahead financially, but for some reason they can never break through to the next level.

- A person enters into a wonderful relationship and everything is great for a while, but after some time has elapsed the spark fades, and the relationship goes from neutral to cold, from bad to worse.

Now there are a lot of reasons other than self-sabotage why any of the above scenarios can happen, but if you find yourself going through similar circumstances in your life, self-sabotage may be something for you to consider. And the first area of your life to examine is your level of self-love.

Ask yourself the following questions:

1. "Do I like myself—who I am and who I am becoming?"

2. "Do I feel that I deserve the best of everything—am I worthy of life's many blessings?"

If your answer to either of the above is less than enthusiastically positive, then you may have discovered what it is that has been holding you back. Self-knowledge is one of the most difficult yet rewarding areas of life to pursue. It is a journey that has no end—an ongoing learning experience that rewards all those who seek it.

Like self-knowledge, learning to like who you are and learning how to become the person that you want to be is a life-long pursuit.

Some areas to concentrate on would include:

- Self-forgiveness and letting go of past mistakes.

- Focusing on your positive attributes and strengths instead of your shortcomings or weaknesses.

- The knowledge that each day gives you the opportunity to start all over again and that the past only limits your future if you allow it to.

- Being thankful for what you do have instead of complaining about what you don't have.

- Not comparing yourself with other people.

- Helping others in need.

- And of course, the grandfather of them all, personal growth.

Personal Growth

"Growth as a couple requires
growth as an individual."
— Darren and Donna McNees

Personal growth is an ongoing process by which you learn more about yourself and how life works. It is developed by actively seeking new knowledge and gaining better understanding, which will in turn enable you to make better decisions and consequently experience better results.

"Cry out for insight and understanding.
Search for them as you would for
lost money or hidden treasure."
— Solomon

Unfortunately, not everyone equates gaining knowledge and understanding to finding hidden treasure. Only one out of seven college graduates will ever step into a bookstore after they leave school. It is said that less than ten percent of Americans will ever read a "self-improvement" book, and only a fraction of those will read a book on how to improve their marriage.

Often, life is like trying to put something together without an instruction manual. Sometimes you figure it out with no problem and sometimes you don't. Sometimes everything works out fine and sometimes it's a struggle. Unfortunately, your life didn't come with an instruction manual. Fortunately, instruction manuals are available— they're called books.

Sure, you can glean excellent information from audio programs, seminars, classes, etc. We use and encourage all of these formats, but nothing can compare to the wealth of knowledge you can get from reading a book.

> "The person who does not read
> is no better off than the person who
> cannot read. The person who does not
> continue to learn and grow as a person
> is no better off than one who cannot."
> — Earl Nightingale

For less than the cost of dinner and a movie you can gather an amazing amount of information and wisdom. In a matter of days or weeks you can learn what took an author his or her whole life to learn.

You can avoid the pitfalls, take shortcuts and accelerate your success because of the research, trial and error, associations and personal experience of an author. Applying this knowledge to your life will improve your odds of achieving success.

It's easy for us to look at a person with a great marriage, successful career or business and beautiful home and say, "Wow, isn't she lucky!" Regardless of your opinion regarding luck, to the outside observer, it does seem like some people are lucky and some are not. Why is that? Let's take a closer look.

- Five percent of Americans control ninety-five percent of the wealth.

- Only five percent of new businesses make it past the first five years.

- Only seventeen percent of marriages are considered to be truly happy according to a ten-year study of thousands of unions conducted by Dr. R. C. Adams.

Are these people lucky? Well, according to Louis Pasteur, *"Chance favors the prepared mind."* Notice that these percentages are in line with the percentages of people who read personal growth materials. In other words, chance favors those who seek wisdom and knowledge. Of course gaining wisdom and knowledge is not enough—you must apply what you have learned.

> "New knowledge is of little value if it doesn't change us, make us better individuals, and help us to be more productive, happy, and useful."
> — Hyrum W. Smith

So how can you become luckier in marriage? You guessed it—seek wisdom. Go to marriage/relationship seminars, hang out with happily married couples, ask for advice from people you respect and read relationship and marriage books. And lastly, make sure to share what you have learned with others.

When you are growing as a person, you feel better about yourself. When you live on purpose and for a purpose you like yourself more. And when you love yourself you have more love to give, which means you will receive more love in return.

There is something very attractive about people who like themselves. If you would like to attract more good into your life, then work on increasing your level of healthy self-love.

Some people believe that thinking highly of themselves is vanity or conceit and that thinking less of themselves is the noble, humble or right thing to do. This kind of thinking is flawed logic or a misguided ideal. Do you believe that thinking less of other people is the noble or right thing to do? Of course you don't. Then why is it okay for you to think of yourself that way?

> "Calm self-confidence is as far from
> conceit as the desire to earn a
> decent living is remote from greed."
> — Channing Pollock

We believe that humility is a virtue, but being humble is not the same as self-degradation. Cutting yourself down or thinking less of yourself isn't humility. The best definition of humility that we've heard is that "humility is not thinking less of yourself, but it's thinking of yourself less." If you were to tell Michael Jordan that he's a great basketball player and he responded by saying, "Oh, I'm not that good," that wouldn't be humility, it would be false humility.

Feeling bad about yourself or your life, being frustrated or even becoming depressed is easy. Anyone can do that. All you have to do is dwell on your faults, past mistakes and failures, think about how much you do versus how little others do or to focus on what's bad in your life instead of what's good. Why live in that negative, disempowering world? Focusing on the bad only brings more bad into your life and self-pity robs you of your joy and keeps you from doing truly great things.

> "What poison is to food,
> self-pity is to life."
> — Oliver C. Wilson

Instead, think about the times when you did something great regardless of how big or small it was. Think about all of the things that you are thankful for. Concentrate on the times when you brightened someone's day, helped someone in need, or gave to a worthy cause.

> "Measure yourself by your best moments,
> not by your worst. We are too prone to
> judge ourselves by our moments of
> despondency and depression."
> — Robert Johnson

Think as well about your strong points—your talents, skills, attributes and abilities. The following is a partial list to aid you in this exercise:

Leader	**Encourager**	**Empathetic**
Teacher	**Artistic**	**Optimistic**

Wisdom	Compassion	Kindness
Hospitality	Serving Others	Faith
Administrator	Good Listener	Giver

Our thoughts and what we decide to focus on are extremely important, but we must not forget the power of our words, especially the words that we use to describe ourselves and our lives.

Thoughts become more real when you speak them. It's as though saying something out loud confirms what you were thinking and strengthens your conviction. This type of negative communication often takes on the form of complaining.

> "When any fit of gloominess, or perversion of mind, lays hold upon you, make it a rule not to publish it by complaints."
> — Samuel Johnson

Complaining has become such an ingrained habit for so many people that they don't even realize that they're doing it. To them, they are just talking, telling a story or giving their opinion. But if forced to only talk about positive and uplifting things, they would find themselves short on words. Now we're not talking about the occasional bad day, but rather a bad habit that's become a way of life.

If you want to feel better about yourself then start by thinking better things about yourself. Mark Twain observed, *"A man cannot be comfortable without his own approval."* If you think poorly of yourself, it's because you have allowed yourself to do so. You have given yourself permission to treat yourself poorly. And since you are the gatekeeper to your mind, you can also give yourself permission to think highly of yourself. Choose the latter regardless of how difficult that may be or how many attempts it takes before you're successful.

If you went on a diet to lose twenty pounds, you wouldn't expect to lose it all after just one meal would you? Likewise, changing a negative mental habit will take time and patience.

Feeling good about you and believing in yourself isn't just about you. It isn't a selfish exercise—far from it. These positive thoughts and attitudes recharge your batteries and refill your "love reserves." The more love, acceptance and patience that you have for yourself, the more loving, accepting and patient you will be with others.

It's also very difficult to believe in yourself if you don't like yourself. And great things aren't done by great people, but rather by average, everyday people who believe in themselves.

> "It's so important to believe in yourself.
> Believe that you can do it,
> under any circumstances. Because if
> you believe you can, then you really
> will. That belief just keeps you
> searching for the answers, and
> then pretty soon you get it."
> — Wally "Famous" Amos

You can change your life by changing your mind. You can decide what you will no longer tolerate in your life. You can choose to believe good things about yourself—after all, they're true.

Thinking well of yourself also has the positive side effect of causing others to hold you in higher regard as well. To a certain degree, we teach people how to treat us. We let them know what is and what isn't acceptable. If you don't like yourself, others will have a harder time liking you. If you don't respect yourself, then you run the risk of others disrespecting you as well. To expect others to treat us better than we treat ourselves is like giving someone a dollar and expecting five quarters in return.

> "The way in which we think of ourselves has everything to do with how our world sees us."
> — Arlene Raven

Perhaps you were told as a child that you were no good or that you wouldn't amount to anything. Maybe you came from a broken home and the instability caused you to become insecure or perhaps you even thought that you were to blame. You may have experienced abuse or didn't receive love as a child and, because of that, you have a hard time loving yourself.

People can say such terrible things, but that doesn't make them true. Let go of the lies and embrace the truth. And the truth is:

- You are an incredible person!

- You have something wonderful to contribute to those around you that only you can give.

- Your past failures do not make you a failure. Not to have failed is not to have tried.

- You have the ability to make your dreams come true. If you have the ability to conceive it, you have the ability to receive it.

- You deserve the best that life has to offer.

If these words make you feel somewhat uncomfortable or if you have a hard time believing them, then this chapter is for you.

As mentioned earlier, in order for you to change your past negative programming, you have to "overwrite" it with positive programming.

The following are some ways that you can rewrite your past negative programming.

1. Read and meditate on positive uplifting materials every day.

2. Every morning when you awake and every night before you go to sleep, read an affirmation to yourself like the example you can find at www.DivorceProofMarriage.com/affirmation.html. Print it out and place it next to your bed or tape it on your bathroom mirror so that you will see it every day.

3. Reduce your exposure to negative people.

> "Keep away from people who try to belittle your ambitions. Small people always do that, but the really great make you feel that you, too, can become great."
> — Mark Twain

4. Spend more time with people who make you feel good about yourself and make new friends who will encourage and lift you up.

5. Reduce your exposure to negative news—TV, radio, newspaper, Internet, etc.

6. As soon as a negative or disempowering thought comes to mind, immediately get rid of it and replace it with a positive empowering one. For example, replace "I'll never be able to do that" with "Other people have done it and so can I." This may be the most difficult exercise you have ever done, but it's absolutely necessary if you want to live an abundant life.

7. Focus on your strengths instead of your weaknesses.

8. Forgive those who have hurt or wronged you.

9. Forgive yourself for past mistakes.

10. Mark today on your calendar as the day that you rejected the lies and accepted the truth. Mark it as the day that you began to like yourself more, which in turn opened up a whole new world of possibilities.

It's okay to love yourself. It's okay to let go of your past and stop beating yourself up over past mistakes. It's okay to want to live a more abundant life. You deserve the best and others deserve to have what only you can give. You are amazing—that much is true. And the sooner you accept that fact, the sooner you will live it.

"Your peace, joy and sense of self-worth
is not a matter of circumstance—it is a matter
of choice. Your past does not exist today—it
only lives on in your thoughts. Your future is
yet to be written—and you hold the pen."
— Darren & Donna McNees

CHAPTER 16

INCREASE THE FUN FACTOR IN YOUR MARRIAGE

"Humor is the great thing, the saving thing. The minute it crops up, all our irritations and resentments slip away, and a sunny spirit takes their place."
— Mark Twain

Having fun is a very important element in truly fulfilling marriages. It is so important that we dedicated the last three chapters of *The 21 Day Marriage Makeover* to discussing its significance and practical application in one's marriage.

Do you have too much fun in your life?

For many people today, that question is as silly as asking if your health is too good or if you have too much money. With today's fast-paced high-stress lifestyle, fun is something that is often overlooked. And having fun with your spouse on a regular basis may not fit into your daily "things to do" list.

Fun is nice and everyone wants to have fun, but how important is it to your marriage? Well, one of the first signs that a marriage is in trouble is when the laughter disappears. The laughter disappears because something negative has taken its place. It could be bitterness or unforgiveness, anger, hurt feelings, depression or stress.

When you're going through a difficult time or if you're under a lot of pressure, isn't it fair to say that you are less likely to joke around, laugh and have fun? Is it possible that the opposite could also be true—that when you joke around, laugh and have fun, you are better equipped to handle pressure and get through your difficult time? Absolutely!

When studying the works of some of the most brilliant business minds in America, we found it interesting that laughter increases creativity and problem solving ability. Laughter, lightening up and having fun can increase your problem-solving skills. Wow—what a great discovery!

This is important to know because problem-solving skills are a key element in long-term healthy relationships. Everyone has problems and faces challenges in their relationship. No one is immune, but it is those who can successfully navigate their way through these challenges who will reap the reward of a happier marriage.

We're not saying that having more fun and laughing more often will save a failing marriage; however, it is without a doubt a very important aspect in a marriage and one that should not be overlooked.

So how do you increase the fun factor in your relationship? That is something that you and/or your spouse will have to answer.

The following are a few pointers to help kick start your creativity:

- **Lighten up.** The many pressures of life can weigh us down and even crush our spirit if we aren't careful. We tend to treat too many things as if they are "life and death" concerns. Lighten up a little and stop being so hard on yourself and/or your spouse. Stop trying to be perfect and expecting others to do the same. Thank goodness perfection is not a prerequisite for success, happiness and a great marriage. This isn't boot camp; this is your life. Enjoy it!

- **Go out on a date.** As will be discussed in the next chapter, a weekly (or at least a monthly) date night is a great way for the two of you to increase the fun factor in your relationship. Try to go somewhere that you normally wouldn't go with each other. New scenery is great for igniting a new spark in your relationship. You don't have to limit your choices to "mature" locations. Go to a park or playground and swing on the swings together. Go for a long walk holding hands. Use your imagination. The important thing is that you are spending time together, just the two of you, outside of your familiar surroundings.

- **Play with your spouse.** If you are a woman reading this section, this is a very important point. As mentioned earlier, there are several specific "love needs" that need to be identified and met in one's relationship in order to experience everything that a great marriage has to offer. For many men, a common "love need" is the need for a playmate. For the most part, men like to play and if they cannot be playing, they like to watch other people play (i.e., sporting events). When you take an interest in his interests, it makes him feel closer to you. And when he feels closer to you, your specific "love needs" begin to be met as well. That's why walking or hiking is such a great activity for couples. His need for a playmate is met and her need for conversation is met.

When you stop having fun, you stop living and start existing. When you take the fun out of your marriage, you lose more than just the fun experience itself. You also lose the potential closeness that can only be gained by playing with your spouse. Joke around, laugh, tickle each other once in a while, plan fun events, chase your mate around the house, etc. When you have fun with your spouse it makes him or her feel special and wanted.

> "Among those whom I like or admire,
> I can find no common denominator,
> but among those whom I love,
> I can: all of them make me laugh."
> — W.H. Auden

Increase the fun factor in your marriage to keep your relationship exciting and fresh.

Have fun and enjoy your life together.

CHAPTER 17

DATE
YOUR
MATE

"Remember that a good marriage is like a campfire.
Both grow cold if left unattended."
— H. Jackson Brown, Jr.

We seem to have become a culture obsessed with "cures." We spend millions upon millions of dollars and countless hours trying to come up with the "cure" for what ails us. More time and money is being spent today than ever before to find the "cure" for diseases like cancer and heart disease, but to no avail. More people are dying of these two diseases than ever before.

The reason why is very simple. Our attention is focused in the wrong direction. We are focusing on the disease instead of focusing on health. Modern medical science has forgotten or purposely ignored the age-old adage that "an ounce of prevention is worth more than a pound of cure."

These words of wisdom have been confirmed through numerous studies, which have concluded that degenerative diseases like cancer and heart disease are eighty percent lifestyle related.

The key to long-term good health is to focus your attention toward getting healthy and staying healthy. Prevention is the answer. The same thing is true with your marriage. The key to long-term marital health is to continually strive to improve the health of your relationship and to do the things that strengthen your bond and increase your love for each other.

It sounds so simple, yet we make it so complicated. Take the physical health example above. It isn't typically until someone is diagnosed with cancer or they have a heart attack that they stop smoking, lose weight, eat better, manage their stress, start taking high quality nutritionals and start exercising. This same kind of thing happens in many marriages throughout the world. Couples typically don't research ways to develop and keep their marriage strong or seek expert advice until cancer develops in their relationship.

It's very rare that we receive an email from someone saying "I have a good marriage now and I want to make it even better. What advice or resource would you recommend to help us keep our marriage strong?" Instead we hear, "My wife just left me," or "My husband told me that he no longer loves me and he wants a divorce—what can I do to save my marriage?"

Don't get us wrong, we want to help all couples regardless of the condition of their marriage. We're just trying to make a point. Don't wait until things go bad before you actively work on improving your marriage. Don't assume that because your marriage is good right now it will stay that way without a continual effort.

Dating your mate is the "ounce of prevention" that you cannot afford to do without.

However, there can be many reasons why couples won't take this simple yet powerfully effective advice:

- "We can't afford it."

- "Our relationship is fine, we don't need to go out on dates."

- "We can't find the time to get away with each other."

- "We enjoy doing things together as a family."

Whatever the reason, the thought process is the same: "I don't think it's necessary."

The following are a few reasons why dating your spouse is absolutely necessary:

1. You'll avoid the "we've grown apart" scenario. It's not uncommon for people to change throughout the years. Our likes and dislikes, goals, dreams and ambitions can change as we progress through life. Dating your spouse is a good way to keep in touch with the person your mate is becoming. Sharing each other's dreams and innermost desires is extremely important, but it's something that is very difficult to do among the many distractions that take place in the home environment.

2. You'll avoid the "empty nest" or "I want to lead my own life now" scenario. When kids enter the scene, they become the center of attention. Much of the conversation and most of the family activities revolve around the children.

If you aren't careful, it's easy to stop investing in your relationship and neglect each other's needs. Then when your children become more independent or leave home, you find yourself living with a roommate instead of a soul mate. A date night helps you reconnect with your partner, rekindle the romance and communicate in a way that lets each of you know whether or not your individual "love needs" are being met.

3. You set a great example for your children to follow. One of the best things that a child can have in his or her life is a mom and dad who are madly in love with each other, and keeping the romance spark alive takes time alone together on a regular basis.

We recommend that you have a date night every week or at the very least once a month. Darren knew someone in high school whose parents had a date night every Thursday. They had four children and still made it a point to take time to date each other. Needless to say, it was obvious that they liked each other. There was definitely something different about them versus most of the other parents that he knew growing up. The reason they were different than most parents was because they were *doing* something different.

Needless to say, the quality of your marital relationship is incredibly important. Make the time, make the arrangements and save the money.

Your marriage is worth it!

CHAPTER 18

GROW TOGETHER BY DREAMING TOGETHER

"Love does not consist in gazing
at each other, but in looking outward
together in the same direction."
— Antoine de Saint-Exupéry

D o you dream together as a couple? There is something very powerful that happens when two like-minded people come together united in a single cause. When you begin to believe that your dreams can come true, hope starts to fill the part of your life where despair used to live.

Hope is a very powerful thing. Hope can turn depression into anticipation, boredom into excitement and a strained relationship into an awesome one.

Get together as a couple and determine:

- Where do you want to be in 5, 10, 15 years from now (i.e. career/job, financially, socially, physically, etc.)?

- Where do you want to live?

- What kind of a house do you want to live in?

- What kind of cars do you want to drive?

- Where do you want to send your kids to college?

- What charities would you like to support?

- What kind of a relationship do you want to have together?

Make dream-building a part of your daily activities. Magic starts to happen when husband and wife dream together.

How can your relationship get stale when you are excited about the future? How can you grow apart when you are planning together? How can you fall out of love when you enjoy sharing ideas and life with each other?

Dreaming together, thinking of life's possibilities and working together toward your common goals will keep your marriage fresh and exciting.

Perhaps having an awesome marriage is too big of a dream for you. Don't let that stop you from doing everything that you can to make it happen. Find other like-minded, fun-loving couples to hang out with.

Look for mentors who will cause you to dream even bigger dreams. Sometimes in order for us to dream big enough, we need to borrow the dreams of others.

Many couples have a great marriage and so can you. It may not happen overnight, but if you do your part and never give up, it will happen.

The following steps can help you in your dream building exercises:

1. Decide what it is that you want to have.

2. Don't focus on what you think you can or can't do, only focus on what it is that you want (as will be discussed in more detail later).

3. Believe that it's possible for you to have it.

4. Go somewhere quiet, close your eyes, and envision yourself having what it is that you want. Do this for at least fifteen minutes every day.

5. Imagine how good it feels. Experience all of the emotions that go along with having what you want. Make it seem real.

6. Write a movie script, in the present tense, of your perfect day and give as much detail as you can. As an example, your movie script could start out like the following:

   "It is June 15, 2014. I am sitting under a palm tree in the back yard of our beautiful new 12,000 square foot dream home in San Diego California. The sky is perfectly clear and the sweet smell of lilacs fills the air. Later this evening we'll be entertaining some of our closest friends..."

7. Read this script out loud every day when you first awake and again before you go to bed. Memorize

your script so that you can say it to yourself whenever you want. Anytime during the day that you have some free time, recite your script (out loud if you are alone and to yourself if there are people around).

8. Know that this reality is on its way to you.

9. Be thankful. An attitude of gratitude is a powerful force for attracting good into your life. Always be thankful for what you already have as well as for what is on its way to you.

It's not a matter of "can do," but rather "will do."

"If we did all the things we are capable of doing, we would literally astound ourselves."
— Thomas Edison

Contrary to what you may have heard, you aren't crazy if you talk to yourself or even answer yourself. What is crazy is not controlling this conversation.

Everyone talks to themselves whether or not they even realize it. This self-talk takes place primarily in our thoughts. And it's the quality of our thoughts that determines the quality of our lives.

Improve the quality of your thoughts and you improve the quality of your life.

> "Sow a thought, and you reap an act;
> Sow an act, and you reap a habit;
> Sow a habit, and you reap a character;
> Sow a character, and you reap a destiny."
> — Samuel Smiles

What kind of destiny are you creating? The answer lies within your thoughts.

The remainder of this chapter deals with one of the most limiting thoughts we all struggle with. This thought is primarily made up of two words. If you can eliminate these two words from your thought life, you'll literally change your life for the better. These limiting self-defeating words are "I can't..."

These two words are usually followed by all of the "reasons" why we can't do a thing.

> "Some men have thousands of reasons why
> they cannot do what they want to, when
> all they need is one reason why they can."
> — Mary Frances Berry

Unfortunately, if you believe that you can't do a thing, then you are right. Your life will become a self-fulfilling prophesy. This is true because of three primary reasons:

1. **You won't even try.** Many people feel comfortable here. They think that if they don't try, then they can't fail. But not trying *is* failure. It's failing to achieve what it is that you truly want.

2. **You will not give it everything you have for fear that it might not work out in the end.** Giving half an effort is a great way to make your "I can't..." thoughts

come true. This is a problem area in many marriages. Anyone in a committed relationship who has the "50/50" or "I'll meet you half way" attitude will always come up short. In order to get 100 percent you have to give 100 percent.

3. **You work hard, achieve your desired results and then lose them.** This can happen because you have programmed your subconscious mind for failure. Deep down you may not believe that you deserve success or you may not view yourself as a successful person. Fortunately, as mentioned earlier you can rewrite this negative programming with positive programming.

There are many forms of "I can't..." that we need to be aware of. The following are just a few:

- "That will never work."

- "What if I try and it doesn't work out?"

> "The only limit to our realization of tomorrow will be our doubts of today."
> — Franklin Delano Roosevelt

- "I'll never be able to..."

- "With my luck..."

> "The champion makes his own luck."
> — Red Blaik

- "I don't deserve to be…"

- "I'm not smart enough, talented enough, young enough, old enough, experienced enough, etc." Getting what you want out of life has very little to do with these kinds of things. Persistence, determination and focusing on what you "will do" instead of what you think you "can do" are what is important.

> "Nothing in the world can take the place of persistence. Talent will not; nothing is more common than unsuccessful individuals with talent. Genius will not; unrewarded genius is almost a proverb. Education will not; the world is full of educated derelicts. Persistence and determination alone are omnipotent."
> — Calvin Coolidge

When people tell us that they can't have an awesome relationship with their spouse because of this, that or the other thing, we get a little sad because we know that unless they change their mind, they're probably right.

Success in any area of life, including your marriage, is not a matter of whether or not you *can*, but rather whether or not you *will*.

Forget about what you "can do"—none of us is smart enough to know what is or isn't possible. Instead, focus on what you "will do" to make your life and your marriage better.

Decide what it is that you want and then go after it with all your strength. You are the only one who can decide what it is that you will do. You have more control over your current and future life than you realize. And it all starts with the thoughts that you allow to occupy your mind.

The next time an "I can't…" phrase pops into your mind, immediately catch yourself and say, "Yes, I can—I can and I will." After a while you will be amazed at what you have been able to accomplish. You are an amazing person with the ability to make a profound difference in your life and the lives of those around you. Improve your thoughts and you will improve your world.

It's not a matter of "can do," but rather "will do."

Think and talk about your possibilities as a couple instead of always thinking and talking about your limitations. Dream big dreams and believe that they can become a reality. Rely on each other for support and never let yourself or your spouse lose hope. Life is a wonderful journey and together you are unstoppable!

CHAPTER 19

WHAT
DO
YOU
BELIEVE?

"You can have anything you want if you will give up the belief that you can't have it."
— Dr. Robert Anthony.

W hat causes a marriage to fail? If we were to all get together and write down as many reasons as we could as to why couples call it quits and go their separate ways, we're sure that our collective list would be several pages long.

Could it be conflict or constant arguing that breaks up a home? Is it financial pressures, job stress, family demands or health concerns? Maybe it's that our wants and needs aren't being met.

Perhaps one or both parties have been hurt or betrayed. How about an affair, loss of trust or lack of respect? Could the break-up occur because they lost the spark, passion, romance or loving feeling that they once had?

All of these reasons and many more can impact the quality of your marriage, but in and of themselves they are not the cause of divorce. They can lead to divorce if you allow them to, but they are not the cause of divorce.

In our opinion, it is belief rather than circumstance that ultimately causes couples to lose hope and throw in the towel. What you believe and what you don't believe can have a greater impact on your marriage than what has happened and what hasn't happened.

You may exist in the physical world, but you live your life primarily in your mind. Now before you roll your eyes and think that we've fallen off the deep end, allow yourself to have an open mind and consider the ideas you are about to read.

We recommend that you read this chapter two or three times today and think about it throughout the week.

Belief is more powerful than circumstance because belief creates circumstance. It is our belief or lack of belief that moves us forward or holds us back. William James stated that, *"Our belief at the beginning of a doubtful undertaking is the one thing that ensures the successful outcome of our venture."*

All of the above mentioned "reasons" for divorce can be considered "doubtful" circumstances or conditions at first glance. And when our emotions are involved, that's when things look the darkest. That's when you need to choose belief over doubt, to live in hope versus despair and choose to win instead of giving up.

"Think you can, think you can't;
either way, you'll be right."
— Henry Ford

We can predict a person's success with a fair amount of accuracy just by listening to them talk. The scriptures say that from the abundance of the heart the mouth speaks.

When people are open and honest they speak what they believe. Here are some examples of a negative belief system:

- "Our marriage will never survive the affair."

- "I don't think we will ever love each other like we used to."

- "Our marriage is beyond repair."

- "I'm not going to try any more. I'm tired of trying to make things work."

- "I think I would be happier with someone else."

- "I've given up hope."

- "We'll always be broke."

- "We'll never be able to dig ourselves out of this hole."

- "My spouse will never go for that."

- "If only my spouse would change, then things would get better."

- "Nothing I can do will make a difference."

- "I guess this is the end of our marriage."

Federico Fellini proclaimed that, *"Our minds can shape the way a thing will be because we act according to our expectations."* If you expect that things will not improve regardless of what or how long you try, then you will not put forth the effort that would have ultimately given you success. And in the words of Isaac Bashevis Singer, *"If you keep on saying things are going to be bad, you have a good chance of being a prophet."*

What caused the great inventor Thomas A. Edison to continue in his pursuit to invent the electric light bulb after over 10,000 failed attempts? What caused Walt Disney to still hang on to his dream of creating Disney Land after being turned down by over 300 banks? What caused Mark Victor Hansen and Jack Canfield to continue pushing their *Chicken Soup for the Soul* book (currently over 112 million copies in the series have been sold) after being rejected by 140 publishers?

They believed in themselves, their dreams and what they were doing. It was a belief that would not die until they had reached their goals.

The saying, "I'll believe it when I see it," is a backward thought process. You have to believe it before you will see it. Continuing to give only if and when you receive cuts off the flow. Trying only so many times before giving up is one of the only ways to guarantee failure. Believing anything less than what you want to happen is selling yourself short.

"You cannot escape the results of your thoughts...
Whatever your present environment may be,
you will fall, remain or rise with your thoughts,
your vision, your ideal. You will become
as small as your controlling desire,
as great as your dominant aspiration."
— James Lane Allen

Belief and doubt are battling for control over your mind and ultimately your life. One will win in the end—which one is up to you.

Doubt enters the scene without any effort at all. Belief, on the other hand, is something that you have to fight for. It is something that you have to take hold of and wrap yourself in. It takes a strong will and a determined spirit to win the battle—to meet your challenges head on and say, "I will not give up because I believe!"

> "No one can defeat us
> unless we first defeat ourselves."
> —Dwight D. Eisenhower

To believe that you are a winner before you have won, to believe your marriage will be restored when you are overcome with pain, to believe in peace in the middle of chaos, to believe in success after numerous failed attempts, that is the key that unlocks the door to a brighter tomorrow.

CHAPTER 20

TAKE
IMMEDIATE
ACTION

"In all human affairs there are efforts,
and there are results, and the strength
of the effort is the measure of the result."
— James Lane Allen

How often do we treat our spouse poorly without realizing that it will negatively impact the quality of our marriage?

How often do we put our needs and desires ahead of our partner's and still expect them to react positively toward us?

Wishing won't turn a strained relationship into an awesome one.

Expecting the best isn't enough to create the life that you desire. Positive thinking alone won't make your dreams come true.

You have to take action.

> "Having the world's best idea will do you
> no good unless you act on it. People who want
> milk shouldn't sit on a stool in the middle of a
> field in hopes that a cow will back up to them."
> — Curtis Grant

Who you are and who you will become is determined by your actions. The relationship that you have with the people in your life is determined by your actions. If it is wise to think before we speak, then we must think double before we act.

> "The only measure of what you believe is
> what you do. If you want to know what people
> believe, don't read what they write, don't ask them
> what they believe, just observe what they do."
> — Ashley Mantagu

The health of your marriage is not measured by how much you love your spouse or how much they mean to you. Trust, appreciation and closeness are fostered through your actions. If your thoughts are the foundation upon which a solid life is built, then your actions are the bricks that build that life.

> "Ideas are powerful things, requiring not
> a studious contemplation but an action,
> even if it is only an inner action."
> — Midge Dector

If your marriage or your life isn't all that you would like it to be, then the first place to look is within. It's easy to blame your past, other people or circumstance for how your life has turned out, but that mindset will only give you more of the same. If you want to experience positive change then you need to take responsibility for your life and ask yourself what "you" can do.

There is a saying that *"The man who has done nothing but wait for his ship to come in has already missed the boat."* You don't have to miss the boat. And if you feel like you have already missed the boat, don't lose hope because life is a long strand of opportunities. Every interaction that you have with another person gives you the opportunity to build upon that relationship. Every minute spent in quiet reflection gives you the opportunity to take inventory of your life and make the necessary changes. Every time that you catch yourself thinking negatively gives you the opportunity to change your mind and focus on the positive. Every day gives you the opportunity to start all over again.

> "The door of opportunity won't open
> unless you do some pushing."
> — Anonymous

Make sure not to wait for opportunity to find you. It is your responsibility to seek it out and make the most of it once you find it. Also keep in mind that we make our opportunities more often than we find them.

> "The only way to get positive feelings about
> yourself is to take positive actions."
> — Reverend Vaughan Quinn

Too many people don't feel good about themselves. Some suffer from low self-esteem because they don't realize how awesome they really are and that they have something important to contribute to this world. They listen to the lies that they tell themselves and the wrong opinions of others.

They long to feel special, like they are a person of importance. What they don't realize is that they are already that person, they just haven't discovered it yet. And that discovery process begins with action.

You feel good by doing good things. You increase your sense of self-worth by making a difference. You feel important by being a part of something that is much bigger than you are.

Every time someone buys one of our books and every time we provide life-coaching or put on a seminar, we feel good about ourselves. Not because we have accomplished something great. Not because we receive money or praise for a job well done. We feel great because we know that we have made a difference. We know that someone's life will be touched because we took action.

The life lived well is not measured by what you have, but rather by what you give. Giving money so that a child will be able to eat tonight will in turn feed your soul. Lifting someone up through your kind words of encouragement elevates you as well. You can't hug someone without receiving a hug in return.

> "There is no genius in life like the
> genius of energy and activity."
> — Donald G. Mitchell

If you don't know what to do, if you aren't yet aware of your unique talents, skills and abilities, then hitch your wagon to something that you believe in, make yourself available and put forth your best effort. While making a difference, don't be surprised if you find yourself in the process.

"If faith without works is dead,
willingness without action is fantasy."
— Anonymous

If you want a great marriage, then *do* the things required to make it so. If you want to feel better about yourself, then do something that gives your life meaning. If you want to achieve greater heights, then you'll have to take greater actions. Whatever it is, follow your intuition and do it now. As Brendan Francis observed, *"Inspirations never go in for long engagements; they demand immediate marriage to action."*

Take action!

CHAPTER 21

NEVER
GIVE
UP!

"Success seems to be largely a matter
of hanging on after others have let go."
— William Feather

We love watching very young children in action. One of the things that impresses us the most is their persistence. If you have young children, you know what we're talking about. If your children are grown, think back for a minute and remember how they acted when they wanted something really badly.

The reason we love to see this trait exercised in children is because it is one that we too often lose as adults — we give up too easily. When a young child really wants something, they will keep asking and asking and asking until they either get it or they are threatened with some kind of punishment.

It's almost like they don't know what the word "no" means. They can hear it 100 times and still persist. All they know is that they want something that they currently don't have and they aren't about to give up until they get it. This is one of the many great lessons that we can learn from children.

Perseverance used to be a trait that was greatly admired in people. No one wanted to be known as a quitter; that would be disgraceful. That is not necessarily the case today. People quit and give up on things all of the time without giving it a second thought. In some cases we are even encouraged to quit—to give up when the going gets rough.

There is no shortage of friends and family members who will support your desire to throw in the towel. Some of them will even try and convince you to do so by saying things like:

- "You've given it a good run, why don't you quit your business and get a job—then you'll at least receive a consistent paycheck."

- "If things aren't working out in your marriage, just get a divorce. Life is too short and you deserve to be with someone better than that."

- "That's a nice dream, but don't get your hopes up. Maybe you should aim a little lower—that way you won't be setting yourself up for disappointment."

We listen to this kind of advice, either from ourselves or from others, and then wonder why our life seems to lack the level of joy and sense of accomplishment that we long for.

Not following your dreams, not finishing what you start and/or quitting when things get tough, all lead to the same place—an unfulfilling life.

> "There are but two roads that lead to an important goal and to the doing of great things: strength and perseverance. Strength is the lot of but a few privileged men; but austere perseverance, harsh and continuous, may be employed by the smallest of us and rarely fails of its purpose, for its silent power grows irresistibly greater with time."
> — Johann von Goethe

Webster's Dictionary defines *persevere* as "to persist in a state, enterprise, or undertaking in spite of counter influences, opposition, or discouragement." Notice that the definition says "in spite of," not "until." The bottom line is this: we all live our lives in one of two camps, the camp of "in spite of" or the camp of "until."

Which camp do you live in? Do you dream, set goals, work your plan and press on in spite of counter influences, opposition or discouragement? Or do you quit when you hit an obstacle or become discouraged when it seems like others are working against you? Which camp do you think will enable you to reach your goals and achieve an awesome marriage?

> "Any man can work when every stroke of his hands brings down the fruit rattling from the tree... but to labor in season and out of season, under every discouragement...that requires heroism which is transcendent."
> — Henry Ward Beecher

A friend of ours sent us the following story which demonstrates the power of persistence:

> "I was just thinking about my grandparents today and something my grandma said to my aunt when I was a teenager. I walked in while they were in the kitchen and caught part of a conversation in which my Gramms said, "If divorce had been acceptable in the early years of our marriage, then we wouldn't still be together." My grandparents will be married for 67 years in August, and both of them say they are more in love now than when they got married."

"Many of life's failures are men who did not realize how close they were to success when they gave up."
— Thomas A. Edison

Let's say that you were given a map, sent on a 100-mile journey and told that your final destination was a really great place. The only rule was that you had to walk the entire trip, but at any time you could send for a car to come and pick you up and take you back home. The trail wasn't a smooth and easy one to traverse. There were many obstacles to overcome and the heat made the trip almost unbearable at times.

At first you're really excited because you're looking forward to going to that really great place. After twenty-five miles had passed, you started to wonder if that "great place" (that you knew very little about) was really worth all of the hassle. But you still had hope that it was, so you continued walking.

At mile forty-five, you are completely exhausted. Thoughts of making the call and going back home crossed your mind more than once. But then you think that maybe the next fifty-five miles will be easier than the first forty-five. Besides, you can't quit now—you're almost half way there.

> "One can go a long way after one is tired."
> — French proverb

After ninety miles, you've had enough. No "great place" is worth this kind of effort and sacrifice. You want to quit and go back home, so you make the call. The sponsors of the journey are very disappointed because you were the 40th consecutive person who failed the test. You see, at the end of the trail was a treasure chest filled with solid gold coins just waiting to be yours as you crossed the finish line. Ten more miles and you would have received over $3 million dollars in gold.

We often forfeit many of life's blessings because we give up too soon. We don't realize that there are treasures waiting for us if we only persist. Are you having thoughts of giving up? Perhaps your marriage isn't working out the way you had planned. Quitting may look like the easy way out, but what if you are only ten miles away from receiving your treasure?

Yes, there will be hard times. Yes, you will be called upon to dig deep and hold on with all of your strength. That's life. When things get tough, it's merely a sign that you're in the race. If things are always easy for you and you have no problems, then you either give up and run away from problems or you simply aren't challenging yourself enough and are living way below your potential.

"Keep on going, and the chances are that you will
stumble on something, perhaps when you are least
expecting it. I never heard of anyone ever
stumbling on something sitting down."
— Charles F. Kettering

William A. Ward summed up the formula for success very eloquently with his four steps to achievement:

1. Plan purposefully

2. Prepare prayerfully

3. Proceed positively

4. Pursue persistently

Without persistence, all of the planning, preparation and positive thinking in the world will get you nowhere. With it, who knows what great things can be done?

Never give up on your dreams, desires and the prospect of a wonderful marriage! And don't stop trying until your miracle happens.

CONCLUSION

"Knowing is not enough; we must apply.
Willing is not enough; we must do."
— Wolfgang von Goethe

Now that you've finished reading this book, you have a very important decision to make. What will you do with this information?

Will you apply what you've learned to your life and your relationships?

Will you actively look for ways to improve your marriage and strive to be the best husband or wife that you can be?

Will you read through this book several times until the principles taught become part of your everyday life—using it as a continual reference, or will you simply put it on a shelf never to be thought of or looked at again?

This very moment in time may very well be a turning point in your life. The decisions that you make from this point forward will determine the quality of your life.

A decision is a very powerful thing. The word "decide" is derived from the Latin word *decidere*, which means to cut off. So, when you make a decision, you cut off all other possibilities.

When you decide to build and maintain an awesome marriage, no other outcome will do. By making that decision you commit yourself to doing whatever it takes to make it so. And that kind of decision and level of commitment will lead to incredible results!

Now go make it happen!

A SPECIAL NOTE
FROM THE AUTHORS

Thank you for taking the time to read *21 Ways to Divorce Proof Your Marriage*. We hope that you found this book to be both educational and inspirational, and we hope that your life will be enriched because of it.

We designed *21 Ways to Divorce Proof Your Marriage* to be your first line of defense against divorce and to help you build the foundation upon which a happy marriage is built. If you'd like to dig a little deeper and discover even more ways to make your marriage the absolute best that it can be, then we'd invite you to visit www.21DayMarriageMakeover.com to learn all about the 21 Day Marriage Makeover Experience.

We know that "an ounce of prevention is worth more than a pound of cure" and we believe that *21 Ways to Divorce Proof Your Marriage* contains the ounce of prevention that we all need in our marriages today. If you agree, and if you'd like to help us in our efforts to spread this message of hope, encouragement and empowerment throughout the world, then we'd encourage you to visit and forward the following website addresses to every married or soon to be married person you know:

www.UltimateRelationshipQuiz.com
www.DivorceProofMarriage.com

The first website contains *The Ultimate Relationship Quiz,* which includes 12 powerful questions designed to reveal the truth about one's marriage. *The Ultimate Relationship Quiz* is truly an eye-opener and a great first step toward experiencing greater levels of communication, addressing unresolved issues, uncovering roadblocks to intimacy and working toward a better marriage. The second website contains information about *21 Ways to Divorce Proof Your Marriage.*

It is our vision to help save and improve over one million marriages by August 2012 and with the help of people like you, we know that our dream will become a reality.

We wish you much success and happiness!

Darren & Donna

PS—We'd really like to hear how this book has improved your marriage and life. To submit your success story, go to www.DivorceProofMarriage.com/feedback.html

ABOUT THE AUTHORS

Darren and Donna McNees are authors of *21 Ways to Divorce Proof Your Marriage, The 21 Day Marriage Makeover* and *The Power to Create Your Future*. They have spent the last seventeen years studying and applying the sciences of human behavior, relationship dynamics and personal success and provide relationship and life coaching advice to individuals, couples and groups throughout the country.

The McNees team has appeared on over seventy radio and television programs and copies of their life-enriching books have been distributed to nineteen countries.

Darren and Donna are passionate about helping people find their purpose and reach their full potential in life. It is their vision to help save and improve over one million marriages and to positively impact the lives of countless others through their inspiring message of hope, encouragement and personal excellence.

ALSO AVAILABLE FROM DARREN AND DONNA

The 21 Day Marriage Makeover
How to transform your marriage into one filled with more love, affection, fun and happiness

The 21 Day Marriage Makeover program is the ultimate relationship-enhancing experience! In it you will discover how to uncover hidden roadblocks to intimacy and experience an incredible closeness with your spouse; the proven way to eliminate your money pressures and create financial abundance; how to address unresolved issues and enjoy more open, honest and meaningful conversation; and the sure-fire way to be shown more love, affection, respect and appreciation.

The 21 Day Marriage Makeover is your proven step-by-step, day-by-day blueprint for marital success!

To learn more go to www.21DayMarriageMakeover.com

"Relationship Dynamics" Newsletter

The "Relationship Dynamics" newsletter is an excellent supplement to *21 Ways to Divorce Proof Your Marriage* and a great way to help keep you on track—and it's free.

Each month you'll receive cutting-edge advice designed to enrich your life and energize your marriage. Filled with proven tips, techniques, strategies and principles as well as a healthy dose of encouragement, inspiration and direction, the "Relationship Dynamics" newsletter is a must-have for every person who wants to get the most out of their relationship.

Sign up at www.RelationshipDynamicsNewsletter.com

ALSO AVAILABLE FROM DARREN AND DONNA

The Power to Create Your Future
How 5 Minutes a Day Can Change Your Life Forever!

The Power to Create Your Future contains 101 powerful life-changing lessons specifically designed to put you on the fast track to a happier and more successful life. Each lesson takes only five minutes to read, yet provides the insight and motivation that could quite possibly change your life forever.

Filled with encouragement, direction, hope and inspiration, *The Power to Create Your Future* is your personal guide to creating the kind of life that you want to live!

Available at www.ThePowerToCreateYourFuture.com

Life Changing Lessons

Whether it's money, good health, great relationships, goal achievement or personal happiness, often the difference between massive success and miserable failure is that one missing ingredient—that valuable piece of information that makes all the difference in the world.

LifeChangingLessons.com is filled with individual lessons each uniquely created to help you find that missing ingredient and enable you to live a better life.

Available at www.LifeChangingLessons.com